WHAT PEOPLE ARE SAYING

Dr. Bodden provides a fresh and thought-provoking look at the subject of leadership. His challenge to spiritual leaders is to truly know themselves, their strengths and weaknesses, and to embrace the tall order of becoming true role models is spot on! He makes a clear and notable distinction between the mentor's transference of knowledge and transference of morals, ethics, and values to the mentee, as the latter speaks volumes and teaches the greater lesson. He closes by reminding us that there can never be success without a successor. So many leaders' lifelong dreams die because of the lack of succession planning. He outlines the necessary steps to ensure that the baton is never dropped but is passed to the next generation. A must read for Elijah's Bread Ministries clergy!

BISHOP J. ALAN NEAL
Elijah's Bread Ministries, Int'l

This book speaks clearly to the practical as well as the internal issues of leadership that are so vital for the development of good, effective leaders. Bodden brings the reader into the world of leadership with its heights of effectiveness to its depths of darkness. There are practical lists here with challenges for action for the leader that are developmental and inspirational. This study speaks with straightforward language to the heart of the issues of leadership including areas needed for leadership development as well as the areas where failure has painted leaders into corners of disaster throughout history. There are examples that enlighten the concepts of leadership as well as biblical insights, and these insights begin at the core of leadership in character and its importance to the leader. The reader will find profound insights, practical applications and inspirational direction for effective leadership and leadership development in this study.

STEVEN CROWTHER, PhD
President, Grace College of Divinity
Adjunct Professor, Regent University,
School of Business and Leadership

Dr. Rickardo Bodden currently holds the post of chief operating officer of our ministry. He has led us in the complex task of transforming our church from an aging, plateaued congregation to a vibrant, multi-generational movement. At every level of service, he has modeled integrity, creative problem solving, and adherence to both biblical principles and current best practices of leadership. You will be helped and encouraged by these pages. Enjoy the read!

HARRY R. JACKSON JR.
Senior Pastor, Hope Christian Church
Bishop, Ambassadors of Hope

Leadership
in the Age of Narcissism

God's Blueprint for Christian Leaders

DR. RICKARDO BODDEN

Carpenter's Son Publishing

Published by Carpenter's Son Publishing, Franklin, Tennessee

Published in association with Larry Carpenter of
Christian Book Services, LLC
www.christianbookservices.com

Cover and Interior Design by Suzanne Lawing

Edited by Adept Content Solutions

Printed in the United States of America

978-1-952025-03-7

This book is dedicated to the greatest mother in the world, the late Norma Bodden. She was the model for stepping up and doing the hard work of supporting her family in spite of many challenges.

Contents

Introduction

Greek mythology tells us the son of the river god Cephissus grew up to love all beautiful things. The most beautiful thing to catch his eye was his own handsome image, and he would gaze endlessly at this reflection in still waters. He fell in love with the reflected image of himself, and that resulted in disturbing consequences. His name was Narcissus.

Millennia later, as the study of the human psyche bloomed, the first wave of psychologists began studying this kind of self-absorption in its many facets. In 1914, Sigmund Freud published a groundbreaking paper called, "On Narcissism," and in it he laid the foundation for the modern psychoanalytic understanding of human behavior.

Humans experience narcissism on many levels, from simple selfishness to a full-blown personality disorder. Narcissistic Personality Disorder is part of the *Diagnostic and Statistical Manual of Mental Disorders*, which doctors use to identify and try to treat the various mental conditions. Narcissism manifests itself in many different ways including, envy, arrogance, a sense of entitlement, superiority, exploitation, and other negative behaviors. Narcissists have little or no understanding of interpersonal boundaries, and so often live in a world of damaged relationships.

The Bible has a broader view of narcissism. In the Old and New Testaments, it portrays narcissism as part of the sinful human condition, and informs us that God-empowered transformation is the only lasting cure. Jesus knew people were naturally narcissistic, and He encouraged them to go against their natures and help others, such as in the cases of the good Samaritan, the prodigal son, the healing of lepers, the feeding of the 5,000, and other selfless acts.

The apostle Paul encapsulated Jesus' antidote to narcissism in Philippians 2:3–5. He said, "Do nothing from selfish ambition or conceit, but in humility count others more significant than yourselves. Let each of you look not only to his own interests, but also to the interests of others. Have this mind among yourselves, which is yours in Christ Jesus."

Sadly, narcissism is still prevalent in the twenty-first century. We see it at all levels, especially in those who hold positions of leadership. However, narcissism is not the way of Christ.

This book offers a practical antidote to the poison of narcissism. It is filled with biblical principles and methods for implementing a mode of leadership modeled by Jesus Christ. In this book, I have tried to apply this leadership model to our present era.

God wants to develop you into a better leader—a better representation of Him, His true image. Simply put, this is a book about leadership development. Your leadership development is crucial, and I believe self-leadership is the basis for all leadership.

God wants more Christian leaders to impact lives and influence culture. According to Matthew 28:19–20, God's people are called to make disciples by teaching and living a lifestyle that reflects the image of Christ to humanity. God is saying here that He has designed the church, His people, not the buildings, to lead. Again we are all called to reach others. That is a call on our lives that will never change.

There are not enough Christian leaders influencing the lives of others. There are not enough Christians intentionally leading with biblical principles. Within the pages of this book you will be challenged to look at the inner you. The focus is not so much on what things we as godly leaders need to "do" but more so on how to "be." This is a basic leadership training manual—a blueprint for Christian leaders and leadership.

Many people do not know what godly leadership is and do not know how to cultivate it in their lives. As you read, I believe you will find answers. This guidebook is filled with solid biblical principles along with practical spiritual and thought-provoking lessons that can be applied to your life now. When put into practice, the information in this book will transform you and others.

God is calling you to be a trained disciple who has matured into a better representation of Him. Do not put off your growth any longer. Discover what it means to be a godly leader and how to put those values and behaviors into practice in your life. No matter your age, occupation, or stage of personal development, God is calling you to have an impact and lead.

The success of any organization rests on its leaders. Allow God to remake you into an intentional and proactive leader armed with His Word and ways to inspire others to achieve their God-given destinies. Use Christian leadership to change the world.

–*Rickardo Bodden*

1

A Staggering Crisis in Leadership

In September 1983, the United States launched five nuclear missiles in an attack on the Soviet Union. Or so it seemed. Lt. Stanislav Petrov of the Soviet Union Air Defense Forces saw the arc of the missiles on his computer screen, and it was his duty to report what he saw. That could have resulted in a counterattack that would have altered human history forever.

But Petrov did not alert the generals. He thought it odd that there were only five launches. He decided to check his computer. He confirmed it was malfunctioning. There was no attack.

As a military officer, Pertov was part of a massive political machine that did not appreciate independent thinking. Leaders had rules in place, and he was expected to follow them slavishly.

But he didn't follow the herd mentality so prevalent in the Soviet Union at the time. He exercised personal leadership, based on his knowledge and values, and he probably saved the world.

What does this mean to you? The worldwide Christian community seems to be under attack. How should we respond? A counterattack, or should we explore other options? Will older hierarchal leadership models serve us, or do we need to rethink the nature of leadership? Perhaps leadership springs from individual values, not organizational structures, as in the case of Lt. Stanislav Petrov. That is the option we want to explore.

MEASURING THE CRISIS

The Body of Christ, and its expression in local churches everywhere, is not in the best position on many fronts. The Pew Research Center, a nonpartisan polling organization, gathered these facts:

- A noticeable decline in the percentage of US adults who believe the biblical elements of the Christmas story, like the reality that Jesus was born of a virgin.

- Western Europe, where Protestant Christianity originated, and Catholicism was based for most of its history, has become one of the world's most secular regions.

- Western Europe, although the majority of adults say they were baptized, today many do not describe themselves as Christians. Some gradually drifted away from religion, stopped believing in religious teachings, or were alienated by scandals or church positions on social issues.

- The share of US adults who describe themselves as Christians has been declining for decades; an extensive survey of more than 35,000 US adults found that the percentages who say they believe in God, pray daily, and regularly go to church or other religious services all have declined modestly in recent years.

- The recent decrease in religious beliefs and behaviors is mainly attributable to the "Nones," the growing group of Americans, particularly the Millennial generation, who say they do not belong to any organized faith.

- Between 2007 and 2014, the percentage of the population that claims Christianity fell from 78.4 percent to 70.6 percent is driven mainly by declines among mainline Protestants and Catholics.

The Barna Group, a Christian organization that does reliable, objective polling, noted other issues that should concern Christian leaders:

- When asked if Christians have a responsibility to tell other people about their religious beliefs (evangelize), most people (54%) disagree while only 46 percent agree.

- Among the American population, most (55%) agree that if a person is generally good, or does good enough things for others during their life, they will earn a place in heaven.

- Pertaining to pastors: 66 percent love to preach God's Word, but only 10 percent love to develop others, 8 percent love to disciple believers, and only 6 percent love sharing the gospel.

- One-quarter of all US adults (24%) generally hold a very favorable opinion of pastors. However, roughly the same proportion reports an unfavorable opinion (28% "somewhat" to "very" negative). One-quarter of the population has little regard for the pastoral influence in their city or neighborhood (23% "not very" to "not at all" influential). One in five adults (19%) consider pastors very influential.

- A majority of current pastors (69%) say even finding future leaders, including to mentor them, is a challenge.

- Most people do not connect the role of faith communities to civic affairs, especially with local efforts like assisting city government, serving public education, doing community clean-up, or engaging in foster care and adoption, and so on.

Other data is just as telling.

- In Canada, Christianity has been shrinking dramatically. In 1970 Canada was 94.5 percent Christian, but by 2010 this figure had dropped to 69.4 percent, with a forecast drop to 66 percent by 2020.

- Agnosticism is the second-largest tradition in Northern America and growing. By 2020, agnostics in Northern America will have tripled from their 1970 percentages. In the United States, their share has increased by a factor of seven. In Canada, between 2010 and 2020, agnosticism will grow almost four times faster than Christianity.

THE TRANSITION TO OUR POST-CHRISTIAN ERA

The reduced impact of the church is not a future event. It has already happened.

In recent church history, there has been a mass exodus of young people. Many Christians, including Christian leaders, have embraced secular beliefs about scripture and reinterpreted God's Word in an attempt to get them to mesh. People doubt the Bible based on compromised teachings of church leaders or the absence of biblically based apologetics. They discard God's Word and then leave the church.

Few would dispute that the Christian Church in Britain is now markedly less popular and influential than they were in 1850–1950. Data reveals there has been a gradual decline over the twentieth century. The decline could rest on things such as:

- Emphasizing membership over attendance as an index of religious interest

- Underestimating the change in the meaning of religious activity

- Concentrating on female piety at the expense of men's involvement

- Exaggerating the postwar revival

The trend across all age groups is to move away from the church because it is not seen as a relevant force in people's daily lives.

A CALL TO HOPE

All the reasons for the decline of the church are far too numerous to cite. However, we can categorize why some, both pastors and people, leave churches:

- Too much organizational bureaucracy

- Organizational demands too high to maintain

- Limited freedom to accomplish personal work goals

- Feelings of being judged by others

- Unresolved interpersonal conflict

- Lack of genuine relationships

This data is not meant to discourage you, but it should serve as stark examples of the work that needs to be accomplished by the Body of Christ to take us into the future. These are examples of what we need to confront for the sake and cause of Christ.

Fortunately, those who have read their Bibles know how the story ends. Christ reigns gloriously, and He gathers the ecclesia, the Church universal, in all its myriad brand names, people groups, and variations in doctrine throughout human history, to reign with Him.

The Church is only secondarily an organization or a building. It is people. We are the Church. That's what Jesus taught us in Matthew 16:18, and Paul reminds us of that in numerous places in the New Testament, like 1 Corinthians 1:2, 2 Corinthians 1:1, Galatians 1:1–2, and Ephesians 5:23–27.

That reality should give us hope. Our role then becomes to be open to the Holy Spirit as a conduit of change. And that change comes through leadership.

THE WAY AHEAD

Christian leaders everywhere are facing discouragement. In far too many cases, they are watching their congregations shrink. That means fewer resources to reach out to the community. Smaller numbers often become unwelcoming, insular groups. Such groups frequently become a breeding ground for unrest. At the same time, non-Christian contemporary values are becoming the norm, and there are fewer people who are willing to bolster the gates of biblical belief against heterodox beliefs.

To undertake such a task, a person needs more than just a call to ministry and or a mere desire to take on such responsibilities. It is a matter of personal development. This developmental process is not just about rules and regulations or affixing oneself to a code of conduct. It is also about spiritual growth.

To be even more succinct, what we need in the church are moral leadership and spiritual leadership, a unique Christian leadership perspective, not one based on refashioned contemporary business leadership ideas.

The reality is, the business world has hijacked some spiritual leadership principles, and we need to reclaim them. We need a true Christian leadership model designed and fashioned by God, for His house, and for His people. It is not enough to try to run spiritual enterprises with man-made secular business models and mind-sets. That often results in trying to mix oil and water.

Of course, many leadership principles transcend secular and faith-based industries and organizations. But to operate in the spiritual niche of accomplishing God's will with the combinations of the spiritual faith and business reason, would-be leaders must keep Christian leadership at the forefront of their thinking and work. The "one thing" principle of Philippians 3:12–14 becomes our beacon as we gain this balance.

Spiritual leaders need some basic blueprints on how to structure the foundations of their leadership and life. This book serves to give the Body of Christ some directional life information. It by no means covers every area a leader needs to know, but it does provide a launch point.

2

The Uniqueness of a Christian Leader

Constantine the Great got his appellation for his leadership skills. He became the emperor of the Western Roman Empire in AD 306, and the combined East and West in 324 after defeating his political adversaries. While in power, Constantine made massive administrative, social, economic, and military reforms to strengthen his empire.

Oh yes, he became a Christian early on. The exact year this occurred is uncertain, but we do know that he continued the use of pagan symbols and act in pagan ways during his reign. He did not submit to baptism until he was on his deathbed in 337. Meanwhile, he made Christianity the state religion, and he even convened the Council of Nicaea (325) to curtail the bickering among Christian clerics. His inconsistent actions should cause us all to pause and think.

What makes a Christian leader? How are they developed? Is there such a thing, or is it just a leader who happens to be a Christian? What separates the two? Does it even matter? My view is that churches, other nonprofit ministries, and

Christian academic institutions should pay attention to these questions as they engage staff or churn out mature disciples who infiltrate, change, and impact the culture for the cause of Christ.

WHAT IS THE FOUNDATION?

To define the core of a leader is to identify and understand the leader's value system. Scott Lichtenstein wrote in, *The Role of Values in Leadership*, that an executive's personal values are a more fundamental leadership attribute than the age, tenure, experience, and level of education a leader possesses.

Personal values can be defined as desirable, trans-situational goals that serve as guiding principles in an individual's life. Understanding why people do what they do compels investigation of the influences that drive their behavior. Essentially, if a leader wants to influence the behavior of others, as most do, he or she needs to understand what is influencing them first.

Personal values keep a leader going in a particular direction. Values can act as perceptual filters that shape decisions and behavior. Leadership is putting forth a set of values and ensuring they are adopted by the workgroup. Only cultures that share common values can create and achieve long-term objectives.

From an organizational perspective, values reveal the organization's culture, identity, and can even define an organization's character. Likewise, the values of individuals in the organization are intimately linked to the culture of which they are a part, both personally and professionally.

Edgar Schein highlighted this connection in his book, *Organizational Culture and Leadership*. He noted that culture is a three-part phenomenon made of artifacts, espoused beliefs and values, and basic assumptions.

- Artifacts are surface-level tangibles and intangibles—language used, preferred clothing, observed behavior, and accepted displays of emotions.
- Espoused beliefs and values are ideals, goals, aspirations, beliefs, and personal mind-set of how things ought to be.
- Basic assumptions embody a person's way of thinking on a deep psychological level. Some ways to define assumptions are what one pays attention to, how one interprets what things mean, and how to respond emotionally to stimuli.

IS A CHRISTIAN LEADER THE SAME AS A MORAL LEADER?

For the Christian who fashions one's life around the teachings of the Bible, values take on an even more monumental role. A disciple of Christ desires to live a life pleasing to the Lord in all respects, not just in rituals and ceremonies of worship (1 Thessalonians 2:4, 4:1; Colossians 3:23). The apostle Paul summarized this in Colossians 1:10. He said, "Walk in a manner worthy of the Lord, fully pleasing to him: bearing fruit in every good work and increasing in the knowledge of God."

This is based on what Jesus taught in John 14:21, "Whoever has my commandments and keeps them, he it is who loves me. And he who loves me will be loved by my Father, and I will love him and manifest myself to him." In other words, the one who values God and follows through with corresponding and congruent behavior is the one who really loves the Lord. The transformative act of loving the Lord produces a new set of values. The core of a Christian is to be Christlike in all respects and in all areas of life. The Christian is on solid footing to believe one is charged, if not obligated, to live out adopted Christian values. It is no different in the leadership realm.

THE ESSENCE OF CHRISTIAN LEADERSHIP

The essence of a Christian leader is found in his or her relationship with scripture. A leader takes Christian values they espouse from God's Word and operationalizes them. They live them to the fullest no matter the occupation or position. That is a genuine Christian leader. Christian leadership is bringing God's ways of doing things (God's kingdom ideals) to whatever arena of life they may find themselves.

Jesus told His disciples, "You are the salt of the earth; but if the salt has become tasteless, how can it be made salty again? It is no longer good for anything except to be thrown out and trampled underfoot by men" (Matthew 5:13).

Jesus was making the point that those who followed would be ones to bring about change, but if they lost that potency (the ability to effect change), they would be good for nothing. Salt (a metaphor of Christian leaders in this case) that loses its ability to bring about a change is worthless.

For further clarity, let's compare two leaders side by side. Both have the same values, morals, and basic beliefs, such as having high standards of personal integrity, belief in the importance of family, and a strong work ethic. One is a disciple of Christ, and one is not. Can one be regarded as a Christian leader and the other not? The Christian leader values and stands upon God's Word as the personal compass that influences all decisions. The Christian leader's spirituality is influencing their outlook, decisions, behaviors, and speech.

The other leader, in comparison, is a person who holds the same rudimentary values but lacks the spiritual foundation upon which the Christian leader stands. One uses the Word of God as a map to guide their life, and the other just uses basic values to steer decisions. Both are good and can get positive results for an organization, but one has a spiritual core of Christ-centeredness that acts as a springboard for action.

In light of this information, can one still be noted as a Christian leader and the other not? The answer is an emphatic yes. The leader who makes decisions just because he or she believes they are good decisions but has no God-centered or biblical foundation for making them is not a Christian leader. Human reasoning alone is not indicative of Christian leadership.

Consider the church at Antioch noted in Acts 11. It was there that the Christ-followers were first called Christians. The name Christian indicated that the assembly there was a gathering in which Jews and Gentiles had become so unique and cohesive that a new name was needed to describe them.

The most unifying characteristic was they were clearly followers of Christ. They were always talking about Him. They were sharing the good news of His power to redeem people from their sins. These Jews and Gentiles had left their previous faith and beliefs (or lack thereof) and chose to follow Christ. These disciples were identified due to their connection with Christ. And the same applies to authentic Christian leaders today.

A Christian leader is a spiritual person because he or she continually nurtures a relationship with God through the Bible, prayer, and godly living. Jesus told the disciples, "The words that I have spoken to you are spirit and life" (John

6:63). One who is merely moral or moralistic cannot assume Christian spirituality.

The attempt to base a religion on morality is dangerous. One concept does not necessarily lead to the other, and both are not created equal. Even accomplishments of an outwardly moralistic appearance are not of the same moral worth.

Take, for example, two men who save the life of a drowning child. One does it out of duty, or perceived moral obligation, and the other does it for the hope of receiving a financial reward. Even morality takes into account motives and intentions. The two men obviously had different motivations.

Likewise, the reason why a Christian accomplishes something or chooses to live life by certain values is in a completely different realm of thinking and intentionality than a moral person who has a different worldview. The Christian moral compass is different from all others because our purpose is to please God, not man.

A CHRISTIAN LEADER ENGENDERS A CHRISTLIKE CULTURE

Leadership obviously affects organizational performance. In his *Harvard Business Review* article, "The Focused Leader," Daniel Goleman said a top responsibility of a leader is to direct an organization's focus. Focus cannot be realized without control and organizational planning, which is all supported by the leader's established and communicated values along with the inculcated culture. Leadership is critical in codifying and maintaining an organization's purpose, values, and vision. Leaders set the example by demonstrating the elements of culture, including values, desired behaviors, foci, and preferred actions in their own lives.

Christian leaders accomplish this by applying their leadership attributes to Bible-based beliefs, values, ethics, character, knowledge, and skills. Once a Christian leader selects and lives Bible-based values, those values will translate into the culture. As the power of salt takes effect, the leader's personal culture should affect the organization's culture.

Once set in motion, an organization's culture can become an autonomous virtuous cycle, influencing everything underneath its boundary-spanning reach. In simple terms, a leader must set a godly example. This is not as easy as it sounds, as we all know. It involves an understanding of biblical principles coupled with self-understanding. A leader must identify the intrinsic driving forces that gives an individual the courage and consistency to engage successfully as a leader.

Identifying deeply held beliefs opens leaders to the opportunity to teach and establish credibility with others. Workers who agree with the culture will validate it by submitting to it. The leadership staff will abide by the values and culture by judging situations, executing decisions to hire, reward, promote, and or fire constituents in accordance with it.

A TIME FOR REFLECTION

Are you a Christian leader? How do you know that?

Do a self-inventory by answering these questions. You may want to journal your answers.

- What people do you value, and why?

- What things do you value, and why?

- What were the circumstances when you sensed a calling from God the first time?

- What events in your life have seemed to confirm your calling to leadership?

- What motivates you?

- What deflates your enthusiasm?

- What positive characteristics is God presently using in your life as you lead others?

- What negative characteristics hinder your leadership that you can improve?

List seven things you can do to help align your attitudes and actions to fulfill your leadership calling.

3

Servant Leaders Belong in the Church

In the late 1890s, a new form of business structure was evolving in the US and around the world. It was called a "corporation." The key features of a corporation are that it limited the financial liability of directors and stockholders, was a legal entity that lived beyond any individual that was part of it, and was governed by a hierarchy of directors and executives.

John D. Rockefeller of Standard Oil was one of the early adopters of this form of governance. It was considered to be a modern, streamlined method of managing finance and workers to maximize profits.

By 1930, his son, John D. Rockefeller, Jr., had installed this form of governance in Riverside Church in New York City, the church the Rockefeller family had bankrolled. The church was nominally Baptist, and they kept some of the biblical terms like "deacon." But corporate form superseded spiritual function. The "trustees" were corporate heads, and they called the shots. This corporate form of church polity spread to churches across America.

But there is a problem. The church of Jesus Christ is not corporate America. Many leaders seem to live their lives and fashion their models of leadership on a secular corporate American mentality. The two are often incompatible and are on opposite ends of the spectrum. When the world says one thing, God often says the opposite. Here are some quick references on how the kingdom of God (how God does things) differs from the typical secular, worldly mentality.

THE WORLD VS. THE KINGDOM OF GOD

Hoard	Give
Hold a Grudge	Forgive
Hate Your Enemies	Love and Pray for Enemies
When There Is Fear	God says Trust Him
Eye for an Eye	Return Evil with Good
Earthly Battles (People)	The Battle Is Spiritual
I/Me Focused	Others Focused
Hedonism	Self-Denial and Godliness

Again, the church is not corporate America. Treating the church as the world is tantamount to the children of Israel being delivered from their Egyptian bondage and then taking their old ways into the new land that God promised them. It will not work well. The church is not the place to play politics for promotion, use cunning to gain favor, use the laity as the way to a higher leadership position, to think of people as a means to an end, or for spiritual leaders to think the people are there for them. In God's kingdom, His leaders are primarily servants.

SERVANT LEADERSHIP IS SPIRITUAL LEADERSHIP

Servant leadership was a concept first coined by Robert K. Greenleaf. It is a philosophy and set of practices that enrich the lives of individuals, builds better organizations, and creates a more fair and caring world. The concept supports that leaders are first and foremost servants and serve followers.

The motivational sources for the leader's behavior are their principles, values, and beliefs as their priority is to seek the follower's gain. The key point here is the concentration and concerted effort is on others and not the individual leader's gain, glamour, and promotion.

The servant leader is starkly different from leaders who put themselves first. The latter may attempt an unusual drive for power or acquire material possessions with the goal to accumulate and exercise power by being at the top of the pyramid or organizational chart.

The servant leader puts the needs of others first and helps people develop and perform at their best. A servant leader wants to share the privilege of power, not consolidate it to serve their own psychological needs.

The servant leader does not love the organization but, rather, loves the people who make up the organization. The people are to be the leader's first focus, and then after that comes the vision, organization, or strategy. A succinct phrase to help capture this point: people are more important than the organization or any particular project pursued by the organization.

LEADER VIRTUE

Being a servant leader is not just a matter of an executive being intentional about doing it, but it is supported by the leader's internal makeup and consequent actions. We call this "virtue." At a base level, virtue primarily refers to a set of attributes that indicates a person's moral status. A virtuous person is one that has high moral excellence. Some synonyms of personal virtue are goodness, righteousness, morality, integrity, dignity, honor, decency, respectability, and nobility.

We are not born virtuous. The good news is that virtues can be developed, and many believe that developing them is what brings us to maturity in Christ. People must be proactive and intentional and ask themselves this important question, "Who do I want to be like?" Once a person has an answer to that question, they must take intentional steps to reflectively and deliberately reinforce the behaviors to achieve the virtue desired. This is how character is built. Kathleen Patterson wrote in *Servant Leadership: A Theoretical Model,* that some of the virtues or character traits leaders need to develop in order to become an effective servant leader are love (*agapao*), humility, altruism, vision, trust, empowerment, and service.

LEADER LOVE

Ecclesiastical leaders who are called by God must love God's people to properly represent God. Christian leadership is a vivid picture of God's image to people. Likewise, the church community is more than a mere gathering of people; it is an instrument for channeling God's saving actions to the world. Love is the basis, the foundation, the cornerstone, the backbone, and the most significant reason for doing anything for God and for others. Sometimes we must remind godly leaders, and ourselves, about this. It is all to love God's people and reflect God's love for them. Consider God's Word ministered through Apostle Paul from 1 Corinthians 13:1–4:

> If I speak in the tongues of men and of angels, but have not love, I am a noisy gong or a clanging cymbal. And if I have prophetic powers, and understand all mysteries and all knowledge, and if I have all faith, so as to remove mountains, but have not love, I am nothing. If I give away all I have, and if I deliver up my body to be burned, but have not love, I gain nothing.

A leader who is supposed to be representing Christ is nothing without love. All seemingly good works are rendered as nothing in God's eyes if love is not a driving factor. Consider the often quoted John 3:16–17:

> For God so loved the world, that he gave his only Son, that whoever believes in him should not perish but have eternal life. For God did not send his Son into the world to condemn the world, but in order that the world might be saved through him.

Leaders show this kind of love by considering each person as a total person, and that includes their needs, wants, and desires.

The New Testament Greek term for this kind of love is *agapao*. It *defines* moral love, which is doing the right thing at the right time for the right reasons.

We can understand this type of love in faith communities, but does it have a place in the workplace? Yes. *Agapao* is the type of love that can operate in any social or moral context. The *agapao* kind of love is consistent with servant leadership because leaders must have a love for their followers as individuals, not merely as members of a group. Servant leaders are willing to learn the giftings and talents of each follower individually.

The leader who leads with this kind of love focuses on the employee first, then on their talents, and finally, on how this benefits the organization. Organizational and department heads must go beyond seeing people as "hired hands" and start seeing them as "hired hearts."

As Christ illustrated by His own behavior, servant leaders genuinely appreciate, care for, and are interested in their people. Furthermore, the servant leader seeks to revere and honor people, as God does, as we saw in John 3:16. This God-like leader's care for others can be seen in the work environment as shows of appreciation, celebrating employee milestones, expressing sympathy, actively listening, communicating, and showing empathy.

HUMILITY

Leaders must be intentional about being humble. When placed in a leadership position, a person is often in a position to have the greatest positive impact or inflict the most damage. That kind of influence and power needs to be carefully exercised. The danger for leaders is that within their organization, the greatest temptation to think themselves superior can be prevalent. Humility should be regarded as not overestimating one's own achievement, abilities, and qualities.

Humility is a virtue that deliberately rejects self-glorification. God detests pride, as seen in James 4:6, "...God opposes the proud but gives grace to the humble."

In this chapter, James is speaking about the problems of carnality (being like the world and not like God). James says

God will resist (battle against) the person who is proud, and that means such people put themselves above others, have an inflated opinion of their merits, and hold others in contempt. On the other hand, God gives grace to the humble, and that grace is protection, strength, and favor.

Depending on which side of the proverbial coin you're on, this scripture can be disconcerting or comforting. This scripture proves that as a leader, you cannot afford to have an attitude of pride and expect the power of God to reside in your life.

Positions of power and influence have a tendency to attract proud and ambitious upwardly mobile individualists. A Chinese Philosopher, Lao-Tzu, noted that before a person can become a leader of others, he or she must avoid putting oneself before others, and to accomplish that by being a humble and supportive resource, not a dominating source. Leader-follower organizational alignment can be fostered because humble leaders proactively give away their power to others. Doing so not only empowers others and strengthens the ability of competent followers, but builds personal and organizational trust and commitment.

This principle is embodied in 1 Peter 5:5–6:

> Likewise, you who are younger, be subject to the elders. Clothe yourselves, all of you, with humility toward one another, for God opposes the proud but gives grace to the humble. Humble yourselves, therefore, under the mighty hand of God so that at the proper time he may exalt you.

Consider these three biblical principles:

• God actively and purposefully resists the proud

- God actively and purposefully gives grace and favor to the humble
- After one humbles themself to God, he promises to exalt them in due time

There are dimensions of humility that can contribute to personal or organizational success. Which one of these applies to you?

- Self-knowledge and self-awareness
- Being teachable
- Acknowledgment of personal limitations
- Commitment to constant learning and improvement
- Dedication to a noble objective or higher purpose
- Acceptance of personal responsibility and accountability
- Willingness to share credit for achievements
- Commitment to the empowerment of others
- Understanding of factors in the big picture
- Recognition of the need to serve others
- Willingness to empower others
- Integrated sense of ethical awareness

ALTRUISM

Altruism is the principle and practice of unselfish concern for or devotion to the welfare of others. Consider the story of the Good Samaritan in Luke 10:30–35:

> Jesus replied, "A man was going down from Jerusalem to Jericho, and he fell among robbers, who stripped

him and beat him and departed, leaving him half dead. Now by chance a priest was going down that road, and when he saw him he passed by on the other side. So likewise a Levite, when he came to the place and saw him, passed by on the other side. But a Samaritan, as he journeyed, came to where he was, and when he saw him, he had compassion. He went to him and bound up his wounds, pouring on oil and wine. Then he set him on his own animal and brought him to an inn and took care of him. And the next day he took out two denarii and gave them to the innkeeper, saying, 'Take care of him, and whatever more you spend, I will repay you when I come back.'"

This story is altruism at its finest. A priest and a Levite did not help, but a good Samaritan did with no evidence of a self-serving, self-aggrandizing, or promotion-seeking attitude seen in this text. The Samaritan did what the men of God (priest and Levite) should have done. This is an example of putting faith into action and being the salt and light Jesus commanded us to be in Matthew 5:13–16:

You are the salt of the earth, but if salt has lost its taste, how shall its saltiness be restored? It is no longer good for anything except to be thrown out and trampled under people's feet. You are the light of the world. A city set on a hill cannot be hidden. Nor do people light a lamp and put it under a basket, but on a stand, and it gives light to all in the house. In the same way, let your light shine before others, so that they may see your good works and give glory to your Father who is in heaven.

This is our mandate. If God's people lose the ability to be salt and light, we are good for nothing. The essence of altruism is that a person's actions benefit another, and this involves risk or sacrifice. The interests of the leader may be risked or even abandoned if a person is to be an effective servant leader.

VISION

A servant leader has vision. It means he or she can look forward and see another person as a viable and worthy person, believes in the better future state for each individual, and seeks to assist each one in reaching that state.

Furthermore, people expect leaders to have a forward-looking sense of vision. The vocabulary may change to include concepts like dreaming, having a forward-thinking agenda, but the message is the same. Leaders need to know where they are going, hence one of the primary reasons why they are given a leadership role. Being visionary is a way of looking at what one wants to be or how one should be.

Paul thought Abraham was a visionary leader and talked about that in Romans 4:1–18. Abraham believed God for the promise (vision) that He gave him. Paul says this is, "calling into existence those things that do not exist." This is what a servant leader does. He sees beyond the present into the future, then develops a plan on how to get followers from the present to the foreseen future.

Robert K. Greenleaf stated that leaders must ask themselves a very important question, "Do the people I serve grow?" An honest and forthright answer to that question could serve as an inspiration or challenge. The organizational team must be preoccupied with the future or rather live with the future in mind.

Constituents need to be served with the future in mind. Vision influences the decisions of the leader and helps the leader shape a plan for the future while asking if the people are being served adequately. They must dream while remaining in the present and focused on the future. This, with commensurate actions, should help foster a forward-looking atmosphere within the organization.

TRUST

Trust is an essential component of the leader-follower relationship. Trust can be defined as a person's beliefs and expectations about how a trustee will behave. To be even more specific, interpersonal trust is the expectancy that the word, verbal or written statement, of another individual (or group) can be relied upon. Trust is an emotional adhesive, a bond between the leader and the follower, and is dependent on the form and quality of the interactions between the parties.

The trusting leader is the one who empowers followers based on a foundation of integrity, respect for others, and service in the organization. Without trust, discord and disharmony can fester. With trust, comes confidence and predictability, which is based on goodwill toward others.

One description of the philosophy behind servant leadership includes helping people to feel comfortable and creating an open environment where everyone has a voice and works collaboratively and collectively. If a leader wants to move fast, he or she must trust people by giving them power with information, then ask them to use it on the organization's behalf. The core values of integrity and honesty build interpersonal and organizational trust and lead to personal credibility.

Leaders are put in positions to solve problems. Leaders exercising influence serve as role models for followers (or other leaders) who respect and trust them and attempt to emulate their behaviors. Jesus illustrated and proved mutual trust and confidence in His followers (team) while He used them to solve problems.

We see this model in the Gospels:

> [Jesus] called the twelve and began to send them out two by two, and gave them authority over the unclean spirits. Mark 6:7.

> Jesus gave them authority (empowered the team) to cast out demons, heal the sick, and proclaim his message. Luke 9:1–10.

Also in Luke 9, Jesus taught the crowd and did not want to send them away hungry. Jesus involved his leaders in participating actively in providing food for the large crowd of people. He used them to organize the crowd and then pass the food to the attendees.

The essential elements of trust are both character (who you are) and competence (the results you produce).

There is a cost associated with low levels of trust in an organization, just as there is an upside for high trust. Those with high-trust levels get more work done, have better results, and win in the marketplace over low-trust peer organizations. In fact, it has been noted that high-trust organizations outperform low-trust organizations by a factor of three.

EMPOWERMENT

There is no servant leadership where there is no sharing of power. Empowerment and trust go hand-in-hand. Empowerment is entrusting power to others; empowering places of work provide workers with access to information, support, resources, and opportunities to learn and develop.

One of the most important reasons to enable followers is the necessity for managers to include their employees to get more involved in the decision-making process.

Only committed individuals empowered with information, and the courage to act, can make a difference in their life and the lives of others. Servant leadership puts an emphasis on service, personal development, and shared decision-making.

The goal of God's leaders should be to make more leaders. We see that principle taught in many places in the Bible.

- In 2 Timothy 2:2, the apostle Paul says, "What you have heard from me in the presence of many witnesses entrust to faithful men, who will be able to teach others also."

- In Titus 1:5, Paul told Titus, "This is why I left you in Crete, so that you might put what remained into order, and appoint elders in every town as I directed you."

- In 1 Corinthians 4, Paul told the congregation in Corinth to imitate him and that he sent Timothy, his son in the faith, to remind them of Paul's lifestyle—the same lifestyle taught everywhere and in every church.

Godly leadership empowerment can and should be cyclic. The leader empowers followers to find their own godly paths, and they, in turn, model the same behavior and are inspired to help others find their best paths. Enabling others involves helping clarify expectations, goals, and responsibilities.

Just as important, it means letting people do their jobs and allowing them to learn, grow, and progress. It means allowing self-direction and freedom to fail; all of this multiplies the followers' strengths and trust. Embracing failure is understanding that it is part of the price of getting an education. It is okay to fail as long as you are failing quickly and cost-effectively, learning from mistakes, and using the insights gained to improve future attempts.

SERVICE

Service is another core component of servant leadership. This kind of service embodies making a choice for the interests of others over self-interest. Servant leaders know they are in the service of others first. Assisting others is more than an avocation in life. It means giving up "self," getting personally involved, being truly authentic and honest toward people, and giving up your priorities. This kind of servanthood is a matter of being generous with time, energy, care, compassion, and possibly even one's belongings.

Service can be infectious in an organization's culture. The leader sets the climate by showing others how to serve, which results in others modeling service in their own style through their own behaviors. This "leading by doing" may seem elementary, but it can inspire and motivate others. Followers under the tyranny of coercive power can often be cruel, brutal, and manipulative. The servant leader's ultimate goal is not to manipulate, but rather create an atmosphere that allows for shared power and autonomy and focuses on stewardship and service.

JESUS, A SERVANT LEADER

Jesus was a servant leader. The primary story that demonstrated this was when He washed the disciple's feet.

> [Jesus] rose from supper. He laid aside his outer garments, and taking a towel, tied it around his waist. Then he poured water into a basin and began to wash

the disciples' feet and to wipe them with the towel that was wrapped around him. He came to Simon Peter, who said to him, "Lord, do you wash my feet?" Jesus answered him, "What I am doing you do not understand now, but afterward you will understand." Peter said to him, "You shall never wash my feet." Jesus answered him, "If I do not wash you, you have no share with me." Simon Peter said to him, "Lord, not my feet only but also my hands and my head!" Jesus said to him, "The one who has bathed does not need to wash, except for his feet, but is completely clean. And you are clean, but not every one of you." For he knew who was to betray him; that was why he said, "Not all of you are clean."

When he had washed their feet and put on his outer garments and resumed his place, he said to them, "Do you understand what I have done to you? You call me Teacher and Lord, and you are right, for so I am. If I then, your Lord and Teacher, have washed your feet, you also ought to wash one another's feet. For I have given you an example, that you also should do just as I have done to you" (John 13:4–15).

Jesus performed a menial task for His followers as an act of servant leadership. Every ecclesiastical leader should realize that there is no job, task, assignment, or duty that is beneath them, no matter if it is cleaning bathrooms, raking leaves, sweeping the entrance to a building before a service, or picking up someone who needs transport. The task does not matter. God washed feet. Jesus fed people physically and spiritually, healed them of diseases of body and spirit, and served the Father to accomplish His will. Jesus died on the cross to redeem mankind (John 3:16; 1 Corinthians 15:3; Romans 4:25).

Jesus put faith into action by aiding others and in so doing was an example for all. Just as Christ lived a life of sacrifice for others, Christian leaders are asked to live a sacrificial life. "If anyone would come after me, let him deny himself and take up his cross and follow me" (Mark 8:34). Christ showed us that the life of leaders is a life of self-denial. Self-denial can be considered a kind of death. It is death to our desires. Often Christians must die to self daily.

Circumstances help us become more like Christ. Curiously, this often happens in the circumstances we don't like. Consider the times you felt the pain of an insult, disappointment, suffering, physical challenge, failure, injustice, or trial, yet did not operate according to fleshly base desires, or non-Christian ways. These are the opportunities to die to pride, ego, sin, or self.

THE ACTIVITIES OF SERVANT LEADERS

Trying to capture every aspect of servant leadership may prove to be a large task. Here are some glimpses of what servant leaders do:

- Providing those that you supervise with the materials and equipment to do their job effectively

- Mentoring

- Coaching

- Providing developmental opportunities related to work, personal talents, or giftings

- Prayer

- Counseling

- Community outreach and service/community social actions: feeding, clothing, providing assistance to those incarcerated and transitioning out, providing shelter, nonviolently protesting against injustice

- Teaching others

- Tending or ministering to people's needs

- Taking care of people above the importance of your bottom line

- Investing in people (time and training)

- Maintain a servant's heart—be willing to do what is needed (no job is beneath you)

- Show others that you are motivated by caring for them

- Leading with these characteristics in mind: Listening to others, be empathic and understanding; support follower's emotional health—physically, emotionally, and spiritually; knowing one's strength and weaknesses; lead by persuasion versus coercion or positional authority, be visionary, and lead by being a good steward

LEARNING BY EXAMPLE

When you think of a modern servant leader, who do you think of? One of the first people that comes to my mind is Nelson Mandela. He was a fiery young revolutionary who tried to make life better for apartheid South Africa, but he was jailed for twenty-seven years by the government for fighting the oppression.

Yet, this was not an example of Mandela's selfless leadership. That began after he was released. White South African

President F. W. de Klerk freed him in 1990, hoping he could help avert a coming racially motivated civil war.

Was Mandela bitter? Did he seek revenge for the injustice? Did he want money and power to calm the social turmoil? No. He worked hand-in-hand with the white power structure to solve immediate problems. And four years after his release from prison, Mandela became the President of South Africa as the result of a free, open, and democratic vote.

What kind of leader did he turn out to be? He emphasized reconciliation among blacks and whites, and the different levels of South African society. He would not allow others to open old wounds. He helped the poor with education and healthcare. In a word, he was a selfless leader.

Nelson Mandela was put in a unique position at a particular point in history. Yet, selflessness is all around us if we stop and think about people in our church or community. Who in your life is a servant leader? What personal attributes do they have that make you think they are servant leaders?

In what ways are you a servant leader? If not, what steps will you take to change? What characteristics would you change first?

4

The Maturing of a Spiritual Leader

Many people hate discipline. It is almost like a curse word to some. What people may not realize is that God expects His people to be spiritually disciplined, and leaders are not exempt. The discipline that God requires is more than physical self-control; it is also spiritual self-control. As an ecclesiastical leader, we are engaged in a constant process of spiritual formation.

Some of the early church fathers put spiritual discipline in a bad light. Origen, Jerome, Augustine, and others emphasized the way John the Baptist lived, and Jesus' forty days in the wilderness, as being a standard for all Christians.

Simeon the Stylite (AD 390–459) is an example of this misguided kind of discipline. He lived for thirty-seven years on top of a pillar in Syria in an attempt to become a more spiritual person. He became a leader of sorts too. He started a trend that lasted beyond his death as many hundreds of others started living atop their own poles.

This seems odd to us today. If there is a lesson to be learned from this misapplication of scripture, it is that spiritual discipline is not painful deprivation. It is a path to joy when we correctly understand that we discipline ourselves—get our carnal natures under control—so we can become more Christlike.

Spiritual formation is an ongoing process of growth but not always in isolation. It often takes place in community with others.

Maybe the reason why there are so many nonchalant, lukewarm, and ineffective spiritual leaders in the Lord's church is that they have not encountered God in an authentic, life-altering way. They are pole-sitters. They have not viewed spiritual formation as the lifelong process it is.

However, to be a genuine spiritual leader, a person must consciously put God in control of their heart, mind, will, and emotions. Their redeemed soul is already the property of Jesus Christ, but yieldedness to that fact is the first step toward maturity.

WHO IS IN THE DRIVER'S SEAT?

Remember, Goleman said a primary job of a leader is to direct the attention of followers. This focus is essentially about concentrating on what is important while filtering out the distractions. The Bible is full of examples where God is giving instructions about what people should do (direction) and how to go about doing it (control). A few biblical examples:

- Control your thought life (Philippians 4:8).

- Respond to situations in a Christlike manner (2 Peter 1:5–6).

- Associate with people who share your values (1 Corinthians 15:33).

This is discipleship. This is Christian development. Taking deliberate steps to follow the Lord's word moves people from self-worship to Christ-centered self-denial that results in positive outcomes.

FRUIT MATTERS

Galatians 5:22–23 is God's catalog of preferred virtues. These are the evidence of a mature disciple of Christ. These qualities represent the presence of the Holy Spirit in the life of a leader.

> The fruit of the Spirit is love, joy, peace, patience, kindness, goodness, faithfulness, gentleness, self-control; against such things, there is no law."

The fact that a leader performs his duties as a representative of Christ carries with it a heavy responsibility. In *The Leadership Challenge*, the book by Kouzes and Posner, they say leaders are to be ambassadors of the values they represent. Their behavior and actions must be congruent with what or whom they are representing. God is saying to His disciples that the fruits of the Spirit are His approved ways to respond to life's situations.

Notice that the apostle Paul says to speak of them as fruit, not mere works because fruit is what grows organically. The whole point of spiritual maturation is empowerment to live in a Christlike way. It is about walking in love as noted in Ephesians 5:2.

EATING THE FRUIT

Some commentators suggest that the nine categories of the fruit of the Spirit can form three groups: spiritual virtues (love, joy, peace), social virtues (longsuffering, kindness, goodness), and guides to conduct (faithfulness, meekness, and self-control).

Some compartmentalize the fruit of the Spirit in other ways. The first three can reflect a person's direct relationship with God, the second three illustrate the Spirit's work toward other people, and the last three reveal the inward work of the Holy Spirit in the heart of believers. Love is expressed by showing proper affection to others. Joy represents the effects of the love of God in the hearts of believers redeemed by Christ. Peace is about a heart that is at rest, secure, and confident in Christ.

Patience is about keeping one's emotional temperature under control. Kindness means the attitude of the heart is mild and considerate to others. Goodness refers to one being ethical, moral, or charitable toward others. Faithfulness is the ability to trust versus being fearful. Gentleness is about the inner calm of a heart that is confident in the love of God. Self-control reflects the inner ability or character trait to be disciplined. As alluded to earlier, spiritual formation is about specifically engaging in intentional biblical behaviors to form soul-building habits.

Christian spiritual formation in the intentional communal process of growing in relationship with God. It is becoming conformed to Christ through the power of the Holy Spirit. Some traditions of worship are a part of the spiritual development process. Some traditional worship practices are prayer, receiving preaching or teaching, praise and worship, confession, ministry to others, and the sacraments. The more a

Christian proactively and deliberately does these things, the more it should become a part of who they are. If not thwarted, the Word of God should be transforming them to be more Christlike in thought and behavior.

PEOPLE WHO ATE GOD'S FRUIT

These spiritual values (convictions) are shaped and strengthened through rituals and, particularly, liturgies. Corporate worship, with its ritual, signs, and gestures, produce knowledge; and a person is changed as he or she engages in them.

Daniel's decision (Daniel 1:8) is an example of spiritual values put into action, "Daniel resolved that he would not defile himself with the king's food, or with the wine that he drank. Therefore he asked the chief of the eunuchs to allow him not to defile himself."

Daniel's actions were dictated by his obedience to God. Devotional and worship practices train the imagination to live well before God. Being a disciple of Christ means that you submit yourself to His teachings and essentially allow yourself to be trained by Him. This training means that you no longer follow your own way.

When the apostle Paul was writing to the church in Rome, he said, "For those whom he foreknew he also predestined to be conformed to the image of his Son, in order that he might be the firstborn among many brothers" (Romans 8:29).

The word to focus on is "conformed." It has the connotation of being shaped. Christlike leaders are molded like pottery. It is not automatic, it's a process of submission, training, and following the dictates of Christ.

Jesus underwent spiritual formation. He was fully God, but He was also fully man and was subject to the will of His Father. We can see the human spiritual formation in these events:

- He committed to doing God's will (Luke 4:1–13).

- He kept in communication with God the Father (Luke 3:21; 5:16; 6:12; 9:18, 28).

- He selected people willing to follow him (Luke 5:1–11).

- He trained his closest disciples (Luke 6:12–16).

- He cared for the needs of his larger following (Luke 7:1–17).

This is the very essence of spiritual formation. The various principles Jesus lived and taught on are covered in the subsequent chapters.

SPIRITUAL DISCIPLINES

In 1 Timothy 4:7, the apostle Paul encourages Timothy to disciple (train) himself by changing his attitudes and actions to conform to godly principles. This is an example of how a person can implement spiritual disciplines in their own life. Spiritual disciplines apply the clear teachings of scripture to daily activity. The Holy Spirit grows His disciples in Christ in this way.

For current and up-and-coming leaders, the new spirituality of today is about doing something to help the world as it is about discovering one's true calling, unique gifts, and being an active partner in service of compassion and justice. These things and more can be accomplished through the discipline of spiritual formation. Having experiences with God is a vital source of strength in one's spiritual journey, and it applies to all generations regardless of the label assigned to them.

Humans create labels and barriers, but that is not the way it is with God. Jesus said, "Come to me, all who labor and are heavy laden, and I will give you rest. Take my yoke upon you and learn from me, for I am gentle and lowly in heart, and you will find rest for your souls. For my yoke is easy, and my burden is light" (Matthew 11:28-30). That is the path we must emulate if we are to be servant leaders.

To be transformed into Christ's image, you have to keep His company; you have to spend time with Him. To assimilate God's personality attributes, you have to be around Him. We see Christ's intended pattern in operation in the early church. Acts 2:42 says, "They devoted themselves to the apostles' teaching and the fellowship, to the breaking of bread and the prayers."

The first responsibility of a person of God is to strive to know God. A Christian leader must think this. Private spiritual fitness is essential to faithful public ministry.

Spiritual discipline should become a habit. A motivational speaker once said motivation is what gets you going, but habit is what keeps you going. It is the disciplined man that will always progess or succeed. Personal spiritual discipline could give you the edge that makes the difference. The difference between being effective or mediocre, or being sharp or dull, is discipline.

One way to gain spiritual discipline is through education. At a fundamental level, formation is the process by which a person learns how to allow God's nature to be in control of his or her life. Receiving God's grace and empowerment is a step-by step-process through which His children are guided, admonished, encouraged, and nurtured to maturity in Christ.

YOUR CALL TO SPIRITUAL ACTION

Spiritual formation is biblical discipleship by another name. To be formed into a disciple, you cannot be passive. You must be intentional.

Each of us must decide to take up our cross and follow Christ. Sometimes it is hard to know how to do that in specific ways. Fortunately, Adele Calhoun wrote the *Spiritual Disciplines Handbook* and listed many components of it. To give you some examples, I have drawn heavily from her list with added definitions and relevant scripture verses for your reflection.

Think about which disciplines you have already addressed and which ones you believe God is speaking to you about to make a part of your life.

- Accountability Partner—A godly friend who is given to encouragement and prayer and is committed to asking the hard questions about struggles, failures, and temptations. James 5:16; Galatians 6:1–2.

- Bible Study—Seeking to understand and apply the truth of scripture to my life. 2 Timothy 3:16; Psalm 119:11.

- Celebration—Worship, praise, and thanksgiving, delighting in the presence of God. Psalm 16:7, 9, 11; Psalm 47:1.

- Chastity—Behavior that cultivates sexual purity. Deuteronomy 5:18; 1 Corinthians 6:18.

- Compassion—Feeling with and for others, extending mercy, and help in practical ways. Mark 1:41; 1 Peter 3:8–9.

- Confession and Self-Examination—A process by which the Holy Spirit reveals what is true about me, opening myself to God so I can authentically seek transformation. Psalm 139:23–24; James 5:16.

- Control of the Tongue—Intentionally being aware and in control of words as well as the tone of voice. James 3:2, 5–7, 9–10; Proverbs 18:7.

- Detachment—Detaching from selfish and self-serving goals (for example, money, power, ego, image, and ungodly relationships) and deliberately forging an attachment to trust in God. Mark 8:34–35; Galatians 2:20.

- Devotional Reading—Growing in relationship with God by reading or listening to scripture, which requires a reflective and listening posture that is open to hearing God's voice. Psalm 119:36, 97, 103, 111.

- Discipling—A journeying process to train, equip, and encourage another to grow in their relationship with Christ. Matthew 28:19; John 20:21.

- Examen—The practice for discerning the activity and voice of God throughout the day, which creates a deeper awareness of God's desires. Colossians 1:9; Philippians 1:9–10.

- Fasting—Denying self of normal necessities or wants to intentionally spend time in prayer. Matthew 6:16–18; Isaiah 58:6–7.

- Fixed-Hour Prayer—Regular and consistent time to pray. Acts 3:1; Daniel 6:10; Psalm 119:164.

- Holy Communion—The Lord's Supper celebrates God's plan of redemption through the sacrificial death of Jesus. Mark 14:22–24; 1 Corinthians 11:26.

- Humility—Let go of self-image/self-promotion and honor others. It is about thinking of yourself less, not thinking less of yourself. Proverbs 11:2, Colossians 3:12; Philippians 2:3.

- Journaling—A writing tool for reflecting on God's guidance, presence as well as explores feelings and thoughts surrounding the events of your life. Psalm 25:4; Psalm 119:18.

- Meditation—Is about giving undivided attention and concentrating on God, His Word, and His work. Joshua 1:8; Psalm 63:6; Psalm 77:12.

- Memorization—The process of continually memorizing God's Word. Psalm 119:11; Psalm 119:97.

- Mentoring—A relational experience when one person empowers another by sharing experiences and resources for personal development and skill. 1 Timothy 1:18; Titus 2:3–5.

- Prayer Walking—Physically walking through an area of concern (businesses, homes, land, schools, churches, etc.) and praying for God's will to come to pass. 1 Timothy 2:1–3.

- Retreat—A specific time to come apart from routine activities to spend time with God for the purpose of being refreshed, renewed, and revived. Mark 6:31; Psalm 46:10; Psalm 23:2–3.

- Self-Care—Protecting and developing the limits (boundaries) and desires of the body, soul, and spirit. Psalm 139:14; 1 Corinthians 3:16; Mark 12:30–31.

- Service—Offering resources, time, talent, and treasure to honor God and to bless others. Matthew 22:37–39; John 12:26.

- Silence—Focusing and listening to the Lord in quiet (no noise or interruption). Luke 5:16.

- Small Group—A regular small gathering to intentionally connect people for the purpose of fellowship and helping each other grow in Christ. Ecclesiastes 4:12; Hebrews 10:25.

- Solitude—Scheduling uninterrupted time to be isolated for the purpose of being alone with God. Mark 1:35; Lamentations 3:28.

- Stewardship—The offering of God's gifts (time, talent, treasure, etc.) to bless people. Matthew 6:19–20; Matthew 25:14–27.

- Submission—Aligning your will with God's will that can include submission to other people out of love and reverence for Christ. Ephesians 5:21; Philippians 2:6–8; Hebrews 13:17.

- Witnessing—Demonstrating and telling the difference Jesus has made in your life. Acts 1:8; Matthew 28:19–20.

As I said, spiritual discipleship requires intentionality. Thus, I urge you to pick six disciplines from the list above and start practicing them today. Make journaling one of the six so you can record and review the progress of your spiritual journey. In the future, you will want to add more of these disciplines as you grow in Christ and expand your spiritual domain.

5

Spiritual Deterrents

Automobile manufacturers have maintenance schedules for new cars. You must change the oil, filters, or have mechanical items checked to keep your car running smoothly. The maintenance plan does not prevent the car from mechanical failure, but it reduces the chances of a major problem that will leave you stranded at the side of the road.

Christian formation is like that. Routine spiritual maintenance saves you from a total breakdown. It involves Bible study, praying, and reaching out to others, but it is more than just actions. Our relationship with God is a spiritual connection, and there are many things we can do to make sure that connection is functioning as God designed it to operate.

There are things that you can do that act as deterrents to a breakdown. Spiritually speaking, God has deterrents to help keep you walking on the godly path for your life.

As I have said, discipline is not a curse word but is one of God's ways of keeping you out of fleshly trouble. Disciplines have a way of keeping you before God in a way that provides you consistent access to God's will, Word, ways, and heart.

Your connection with God is a deterrent to a breakdown that inevitably ends in a return to a fleshly life.

If you are consumed with fulfilling His heart, you will not be so quick to fulfill the base desires of the flesh. Why? Because you are being conformed into Christ's image. Spiritual formation (discipline) will not guarantee that you will not deliberately make the wrong decisions, have a moral failure, or live with major lapses of integrity. However, submitting to God's developmental process of continual growth by an act of your will puts preventative maintenance measures in place. Even if there is a problem, you'll find it easier to get back on track if you have been following God's prescribed maintenance plan as it is revealed in the Bible.

There are many disciplines that are available to the follower of Christ. Each person must choose which specific disciplines they will use in their life. The choice may be based on a personal decision, a specific requirement from submission to a leader or leadership model, or as directed by inspiration from the Holy Spirit. Again, disciplines can not only form one's spiritual life, but keep and improve it.

A LIFE OF DISCIPLINE

Ecclesiastical leaders should not limit a disciplined life to the spiritual matters discussed so far. It needs to be more than a "to-do" list. It needs to be a principle leaders live and lead by. Discipline should be a life-influencing value. Godly and balanced regimentation must be ingrained in every leader's life.

In *The Disciplined Life*, Richard S. Taylor wrote that personal power is based on being disciplined. The dedicated and orderly mind will have an advantage over the scatter-brained person.

Besides the common understanding of discipline, there are a couple of other definitions to broaden your understanding of what God is communicating to you. Discipline is the steady application of particular ways of thinking and behaving that are crucial for one to succeed. According to Taylor, self-discipline is the ability to control conduct by principle and judgment rather than impulse, desire, pressure, or social tradition.

The goal for every leader should be to have a disciplined character. The disciplined mind and body are adjuncts and outflows of a disciplined character. Taylor stated the disciplined character belongs to the person who achieves balance by bringing all his or her faculties and powers under control. Discipline is not just related to control; it is control. Discipline is a habit. Furthermore, habit is *controlled self-leadership.*

Self-control enables true excellence. The structured and consistent make sacrifices that are required, and they do not fear self-denial. Relatively few are willing to pay the price for self-mastery.

John Manning, in *The Disciplined Leader: Keeping Focus on What Really Matters,* stated that self-controlled people consistently adhere to specific ways of thinking and behaviors that ultimately develops and guides them.

A disciplined person's order, consistency, and purpose empower them to:

- Have inward resources and personal reserves, which the undisciplined do not have
- Stanchly face their duty
- Be led by a personal sense of responsibility

- Have character that carries them into positions of larger responsibility

Manning believes disciplined leaders focus on three core areas:

- Leading themselves
- Leading their teams
- Leading their organizations

That order is significant. Disciplined leaders consistently focus on what really matters, and that is the people. These leaders align their habits and practices to their beliefs. Again, spiritual disciplines should permeate the leader's whole life.

THE MATURE DISCIPLE

Those charged with the responsibility to lead people need to be highly proficient at how to subordinate. Essentially this is the ability to adjust behavior to maintain self-control. Taylor discusses several areas that illustrate the disciplines of a mature disciple.

APPETITES

Leaders must suppress their fleshly appetites when they conflict with God's will, Word, and ways. The appetites should serve the mind that is ultimately led by Christ. Paul said in 1 Corinthians 9:27 that he disciplined his body to keep it under control.

No leader should be driven by bodily desires for food, sex, or any other base desire. Yes, God has provided these things for people to enjoy all within the confines of godliness and control. All Christians, whether leaders or not, are to be led by the Spirit and not by their carnal nature.

EMOTIONS

Far too many people are led and driven by their emotions. A department head that is constantly moody does not present a good example for others to follow. Taylor stated that emotions should be subordinate to reason. Using the excuse like, "I lashed out because I was mad" or "I did it because I was furious" are not the comments of a person who has their own soul under godly control. An undisciplined soul leads to undisciplined emotions and words.

The soul needs to be cleansed and kept on the leash of discipline. Then, and only then, can it be partnered with the godly mind to live according to God's Word. Leaders do not allow themselves to be led by fleeting impulses. People of disciplined character keep appropriate emotional boundaries with others, and that enhances relationships. A person cannot always control how they feel, but they can control their actions when they are disciplined.

MOODS

Leaders should not be moody. A person's mood is bound to change in light of various factors, but leaders should be steady in mood and not be seen as being tossed to and fro by the wind of emotion. A mood change is no excuse to choose unrighteous or inappropriate actions. Do not cater to moodiness. Everyone can experience mood swings, but do not let the swings be the source of inappropriate actions.

SPEECH

Leaders must restrain their tongues. Having a controlled will, body (appetites), and mind (thought life) is not enough. Psalm 141:3 should be the prayer of every leader, "Set a guard, O Lord, over my mouth; keep watch over the door of my lips!" The tongue reveals a flawed character.

Christians ought not to live by the notion of, "I will say whatever I want to say whenever I want to say it." The scripture that supports this folly-filled mind-set is Proverbs 29:11, "A fool gives full vent to his spirit, but a wise man quietly holds it back." Taylor stated that frankness could be a virtue when it is tied with intelligence, tact, and discretion. It is terrible for a leader to have vocal eruptions like a spewing volcano with no regard for time, place, or feelings. Leaders must execute wisdom with their mouths.

PRIORITIES

Leaders should be highly proficient in setting priorities. One of the chief jobs of leadership is to determine what is important. Setting the agenda is the responsibility of those in charge. Leaders know what things can come before others. For example, God's people come before money and projects. Paying the important bills should always come before low priority and unimportant wants. Ecclesiastical leaders know that soul-winning and righteousness come before many other unnecessary wishes.

Priorities should match what the leader values. The zenith of this kind of maturity is seen in day-to-day activities and decisions. Priorities are about rejecting some things over others. Priorities are about eliminating that which is of lesser importance. What you select to do can either show your leadership and intellectual prowess or lack of it.

HOW TO BECOME A DISCIPLINED PERSON

Living the Christlike life requires deliberate action and a fixed mind of dedication to the Spirit of God. It assumes that the leader understands that God has a plan, and the leader is to discern and act on it. Thus, discipline contributes to a leader's long-term success.

Below are some suggestions on how leaders can become more self-controlled. Always remember, being a disciplined person is accomplished by learned and practiced behavior and is implemented through the power of God's Spirit.

- Buffet yourself. Taylor noted that Christlikeness should always be the goal of life, not the relentless pursuit of plea-sure-seeking. Christians are not hedonistic. Yes, God has given us things to enjoy, and we should, but enjoyment and pleasure-seeking should not drive one's behavior past God-designed boundaries as outlined in Matthew 16:24, Mark 8:34, and Luke 9:23.

- Eliminate Enticements. Let's say you are on a new eat-ing plan that has no allowances for dairy or sweets. But you enjoy dairy and sweets and have a hard time resist-ing them. One of the easiest things to do is to remove all dairy and sugary sweets from your home. Removing the temptations in advance is another way of harnessing impulses.

- Pay attention to the small things. Regimentation as a leader is not just about wielding personal and professional power appropriately in board meetings or about influencing groups of people. One becomes more disciplined by the small daily things like making the bed, folding and putting away laundry, replacing things to their proper location, and other such things. These kinds of small details make a big difference in your outlook, and they affect all aspects of your life.

- Keep Fit. Your body is important. You get multiple benefits from a healthy diet and exercise that extends beyond the physical aspect. Exercise enhances your emotional well-being too. Still, the mind and focus the body to accomplish God's will for you and your organization.

- Do Not Make a Habit of Quitting. Repeatedly quitting things such as programs, jobs, and tasks can become a part of your character if you let it be. Embrace hard issues and deal with them as well as you can. Use tools like counsel and research to help you to solve them. Consider going after difficult things first instead of leaving them for last. Do not be a procrastinator. Be an effective steward of your time.

- Be on Time. Everyone may be late sometimes. But making lateness a habit is rude and disrespectful to others. It can give the impression that the late person's time is more important than others. Leaders especially need to plan ahead when they need to be somewhere. To avoid lateness, some live by the phrase, "If you are not early, you are late."

- Focus. Focus is about directing your own attention to what is paramount at the moment. Focus is about filtering out distractions and prioritizing what needs to be done.

Focus brings all your faculties (body, mind, will, and emotions) to bear on a situation. Rid your mind of clutter and give no attention to fleeting impulses. Set boundaries to curtail outside interruptions.

- Be Resilient, Not Rigid. You can be disciplined and still be spontaneous and able to change at a moment's notice. Leaders need to adjust as circumstances change. Discipline is about being resilient in the face of change.

- Listen to Your Critics. If there is a specific criticism that you consistently receive, regardless of how it was given or the source, consider that it may be valid. Be willing to learn from all people, both those you admire and those you may sometimes think of as a thorn in your flesh. God will use all kinds of people to help keep you on his path.

- Be Responsible. Disciplined leaders honor their commitments. That, of course, includes commitments to God, marriage, family, occupation, and the people of this world with whom you come in contact. Relationships and obligations such as these require loyalty, support, your presence of mind, and very often your physical presence.

WHERE WILL THIS LEAD YOU?

These are praiseworthy paths to becoming a disciplined leader. The challenge is putting them into action. No matter how spiritually minded you may be, or how much you want to touch the lives of others as Christian leaders, you must keep your spiritual training in perspective.

Peter was perhaps the most zealous follower of Jesus. He was attentive to the message of Jesus and attempted to do as his Master said. Jesus recognized that and identified him as being the bedrock of the church.

Peter was imperfect as we all know. Even though he was rubbing shoulders with God incarnate, had seen the miracles and the healings, he was not above looking out for his own skin. At night in the courtyard, Peter denied his Lord three times just as Jesus predicted.

At that moment, Peter realized that he had bitten off more than he could chew. He was filled with spiritual knowledge and aspired to spiritual power, but he still did not have the discipline to stand by Jesus at a crucial moment in the unfolding of the gospel story.

What am I saying here? I want to draw a parallel between our human desire to lead and our shortcomings when it comes to discipline. Jesus understands that discipleship is a process and not an event. Nevertheless, within the process there are many events, and the ten listed previously are part of that path to Christian maturity.

Therefore, I'd like to suggest that you not try to implement these ten steps at one time. If you do, you may experience spiritual overload as Peter did. Instead, I suggest that you spend an entire week on the spiritual exercise of "buffeting yourself." The next week, add the discipline of "eliminating enticements" to it and concentrate on it while still buffeting yourself.

The third week, you want to focus on, "paying attention to the small things," while still buffeting yourself and eliminating enticements.

This method will enable you to build a strong wall of discipline, brick upon brick until you discover you have the spiritual skills to meet particular situations in spiritually disciplined ways.

Who knows, you may find yourself in a courtyard one dark night, and someone may point a finger at you and say, "That person was with Him!" With the kind of spiritual discipline I'm speaking about here, you'll be able to look up and say, "Yes, I was with Him." When a Christian leader is disciplined, he or she enters a whole new era of discipleship, the kind of discipleship that is contagious.

Understand that becoming a spiritual person takes effort, and you must take practical steps to do it, especially in areas that you are the most undisciplined. When you change your thoughts, you change your life. There are no shortcuts when it comes to discipline.

6

Self-Leadership–
Know Yourself

If you're a frequent flyer, you are familiar with the speech that a member of the cabin crew gives on each flight. The crew member goes through a choreographed demonstration of what to do if the cabin depressurizes and the oxygen masks drop. They demonstrate how to place them over your nose and mouth and keep breathing until the pilot gives the all-clear announcement.

Along with this announcement should include one very important point. That is, if you're flying with a child, you should place the oxygen mask over your own face first before you attempt to help your child with his or her mask.

That seems like a narcissistic thing to do. Almost no parent would put their own needs before the needs of their child. It would seem to be a selfish act to many.

The reality is, putting on your own mask before trying to help your child is a positive act of self-leadership. A parent would need a disciplined mind to do it.

Why do safety officials say that a parent should put on his or her own oxygen mask first? Because without oxygen, the parent may black out before they have the opportunity to help their child.

Likewise, leaders can be so absorbed with the needs of others that they fail to assess their own needs. They suddenly find themselves gasping for breath because they have skewed their priorities. They have failed to understand and develop self-leadership.

Self-leadership is the practice of influencing yourself. In a paper written by Marco Furtner, John Rauthmann and Pierre Sachse, "Unique Self-Leadership: A Bifactor Model Approach," they describe it as being supported by three distinct fields:

- Behavior-focused strategies (self-goal setting, self-reward, self-punishment, and self-observation)

- Natural reward strategies (being so motivated to focus on the good or pleasant parts of a task that when accomplished become self-rewarding)

- Constructive thought pattern strategies (visualizing successful performance, self-talk, evaluating one's beliefs and assumptions)

Another way to describe self-leadership is the continual process of intentionally and proactively influencing your own thinking, behaviors, and feelings to achieve your goals. In even more simplified terms, self-leadership is about being able to make a plan, create a list of tasks, and being self-motivated enough to accomplish them without being micromanaged by anyone.

This brand of leadership is often tied to self-efficacy. Self-efficacy is about believing in your own abilities, capabilities, and exercise of control, and that influences how you go about accomplishing goals.

Here is what self-leadership is not:

- Being independent, being your own island
- Never needing help
- Being too proud to ask for assistance

These things have nothing to do with leadership.

Self-leadership is someone who is intentional or otherwise being proactive. A leader with a proactive nature has a tendency to show initiative and take action in order to effect meaningful change. Individuals with a proactive personality identify opportunities and act on them, show initiative (self-starter), and persevere until meaningful change occurs.

GET TO KNOW YOURSELF

Psalm 103:14 tells us that God knows our frame. He knows your essential nature, body, mind, spirit, and purpose.

The big question is, do you know this for yourself?

What is your frame? What is your internal makeup? To be an effective leader and exercise self-leadership, you need to know yourself on a deep level. This is self-awareness, and involves knowing:

- What you are good at (strengths)
- What you are not so good at (weaknesses)
- What your talents/gifts are (naturally and spiritually)
- Your personality type
- If you are an introvert or extrovert
- What you like

- What you hate
- What are the values you live by (what's important to you)
- Your preferred leadership style(s)
- Your life's purpose (why you are here)
- What motivates you
- How others perceive you

The point is, it may be more difficult to lead others if you do know who you are as a person. For example, if you know you are not good with people, then stop seeking positions where that interpersonal strength is needed. Don't allow others to place you in those positions. In a typical church worship construct, if you are not good at connecting with people, despise talking with others, hate to lead teams, and you are just socially awkward around others, then you probably should not serve as a lead pastor or teacher.

THE EMERGING SELF

I am not referring to areas in your life that you may be currently weak in, and that can be enhanced with training and opportunity.

I am not referring to giftings and abilities in you that may currently be lying dormant. I am referring to competencies and traits that are just not in you, and unless God does a miracle, you will never have.

If you hate numbers and hate working with calculations, processes, forms, timelines, and are not detailed, you may not be the best fit to be an accountant. Nor should you want to be. Knowing who you are can help you avoid the minefield of making major mistakes and just outright failing unnecessarily.

People endowed by God with the gift of leadership (Romans 12:8) should take responsibility (being mindful of what is required of them) for all that is under their charge and take the initiative. Imagine the efficiency of a company, ministry, church, or faith-based business if all the associates or employees practiced this way of thinking and living. Self-leaders step up and ask for the things that they need.

These leaders, for the most part, can manage themselves. It is about having the attitude and the skillset for proactively obtaining resources you need to accomplish your goals. No one is an expert at everything, so self-leaders ask for help when needed. But you have to know about yourself to know who you are and who you are not.

GOD-MOTIVATED, SELF-ACTUATED

Self-leadership is essentially leading from the inside out. You cannot overlook your personal life. To do so is a disservice to yourself. You cannot and must not neglect your personal life. Our personal life is the core of our life. Your personal life will affect your outer or public leadership.

The apostle Paul took this seriously. He said, "I discipline my body and keep it under control, lest after preaching to others I myself should be disqualified" (1 Corinthians 9:27).

When Paul spoke of disciplining his body, he was not talking about getting exercise. The word used here for "body" is *soma*, and that word relates to a person's entire being, the totality of who they are, body, soul, and spirit.

Discipline in this scripture means to handle the body roughly or discipline it by hardships. Control means to treat the body with severity or subject it to stern and rigid discipline.

This scripture speaks to self-leadership, spiritual formation, and spiritual discipline.

Paul understood that he was an example and that he would transform himself to be what was needed to win others to Christ. Consider this broader section of scripture (1 Corinthians 9:19–27) for a more comprehensive understanding.

> For though I am free from all, I have made myself a servant to all, that I might win more of them. To the Jews, I became as a Jew, in order to win Jews. To those under the law I became as one under the law (though not being myself under the law) that I might win those under the law. To those outside the law I became as one outside the law (not being outside the law of God but under the law of Christ) that I might win those outside the law. To the weak I became weak, that I might win the weak. I have become all things to all people, that by all means I might save some. I do it all for the sake of the gospel, that I may share with them in its blessings. Do you not know that in a race all the runners run, but only one receives the prize? So run that you may obtain it. Every athlete exercises self-control in all things. They do it to receive a perishable wreath, but we an imperishable. So I do not run aimlessly; I do not box as one beating the air. But I discipline my body and keep it under control, lest after preaching to others I myself should be disqualified.

Eric Rust, in an article entitled "Self-Leadership: Leading From the Inside Out," noted that leaders must care for, cultivate, and manage their personal lives. He also noted that self-leadership needs to occupy a hefty 50 percent of a leader's time in order to gain self-mastery.

Rust also noted these six guidelines that have a direct application to self-leadership, spiritual formation, and discipline.

- Take the time for consistent reflection and restoration of body and soul. Life can be so fast-paced that leaders find little time for themselves.

  Our premier example, Jesus, modeled soul restoration and maintenance by routinely leaving the crowds to spend time alone with the Father (Matthew 14:23; Luke 5:16; Luke 6:12; Luke 9:18). Self-leaders create time on a regular basis to pray, journal, and read (as spiritual formation and spiritual disciplines). A well-ordered heart is the best gift a leader can give his followers.

  In addition, leaders should take care of their bodies, which is a natural or physical discipline. Physical health should not be a blind spot for spiritual leaders. Consider 1 Corinthians 6:20 that states we are to glorify God in our bodies. It is common sense that good health provides the energy and stamina to pursue God's will. In plain terms, eating well and exercising regularly should be a part of every leader's lifestyle.

- Remember, you are an example and an ambassador of God. That must be at the forefront of your mind when faced with an ethical choice or a temptation. Think of all those who are watching, inspecting, or even surveilling your lifestyle. That includes children, friends, mentees, and fellow Christians and non-Christians. What are the second- and third-order effects of your decisions? How will your decisions impact yourself and them? Always strive for the moral high ground.

- Consider being accountable to a small group of trusted friends as a spiritual discipline. Why? Lone Ranger saints (isolated leaders) risk burnout more than leaders who are in relationships that provide accountability and godly counsel. Self-leadership does not mean you should go it alone. It means you are self-directed to make good choices. It's a good thing to check in with colleagues regularly where you have the freedom to ask and answer the deeper questions of lifestyle, leadership, and relationship with Christ.

- Cultivate your inner life by focusing on integrity without being self-righteous or judgmental. Discover what it means to be an authentic Christian person. The challenge of authenticity is being true and real to ourselves and to others.

- Grow deep in your own faith, completely outside the context of your leadership role. As Christ's disciples, we believe the Holy Spirit has the power to bring about spiritual change to the hearts of men. Our character development is too difficult a task for us to accomplish without God's help. The deeper you go into God's love, the deeper our love for others becomes.

- Deal firmly, uncompromisingly, and proactively with character flaws and hidden sin. Christians who are self-leaders are not excuse-makers. Some leaders have self-control issues, such as anger, or can have codependent tendencies. These issues will affect a leader's ability to lead. Spiritual leaders must work on their issues, as the strength of the Body of Christ largely rests on its leaders.

WHAT IS YOUR DARK SIDE?

All people have a dark side. These dark sides can vary in severity and type. Some are people-pleasers, while others desire to build a name for themselves.

According to Gary McIntosh and Samuel Rima, the authors of *Overcoming the Dark Side of Leadership*, the term *dark side* refers to a person's inner urges, compulsions, and personality dysfunctions that frequently go unexamined or remain unknown until there is an emotional explosion. A significant problem usually causes a person to stop and try to figure out why they have acted as they have.

The term *dark side* is also used because it is already a part of each of us. We are often unaware of the hidden things in our personality. The dark side has a duplicitous nature that can be both positive and negative. The same internal issues can foster you to be successful or circumvent your success.

All mankind is flawed. Jeremiah, the prophet, said, "The heart is deceitful above all things, and desperately sick" (Jeremiah 17:9).

In Romans 3:23, Paul told the Christians in Rome that all people have sinned (missed or wandered from the path of uprightness, to do or go wrong; violated God's law) and fallen short of God's glory.

Part of the insidious nature of our dark side is that it is often unknown to us. We are blind to our weaknesses. There are numerous factors that contribute to the development of an individual's dark side. Some causes or contributing factors are:

- How a person is raised

- Their response to being abused, overlooked, or rejected

- Over-inflated ambition

- Being a people pleaser
- Being too controlling
- Being a perfectionist
- Irrational fears
- Fear of failing
- Drug abuse

These are just a few examples. The main point is that any behavior that controls a person, any compulsion (urge), or motivation that uncontrollably drives a person, is a possible sign of the dark side's presence.

To add a measure of balance, the dark side can be used to serve God's purposes for your life or used to serve your unmet needs. It all depends on how you deal with it. Again, this relates to the two-sided nature of the dark side.

If you have experienced rejection and being overlooked by those in significant positions in your life, this could spur you on the path to being a great leader that pays attention and properly guides the people that are under your responsibility.

Experiencing suffering by the hands of an abusive father could be the motivation for you to be a loving, godly parent. Again it is all in how you respond. The goal for any Christian is to be Spirit-led and to reject the carnal inclinations that dwell within us.

UNDERSTANDING THE DARK TRIAD

In psychological studies, there is something called The Dark Triad. This triad represents three groups of socially undesirable traits. The three are:

- Subclinical narcissism

- Machiavellianism

- Subclinical psychopathy

These three groups share similarities but are distinct socially averse behaviors to look out for. Each group includes but is not limited to certain behaviors.

If you identify them as part of your own psychological makeup, you need to consider to what degree these characteristics define the way you think, how you react to situations, and ultimately if they manifest in your lifestyle and leadership.

The detailed list below is not necessarily an all-encompassing list of mental and behavioral traits, but it does provide a foundation for identification. Do you see any characteristics that resemble you or how others view you? Do you see these attributes in other leaders?

Machiavellianism	Narcissism	Psychopathy
Deceptive	Arrogant/Vain/Conceited	Anti-social
Emotionally Detached	Attention Seeking	Arrogant
Exploitative	Entitled	Callous/Uncaring
Flatters Others	Exploitative	Deceitful
Manipulative	Grandiose	Selfish
Self-interest	Self-focused	Shallow Personality

In their paper, "The Dark Triad and Normal Personality Traits," Sharon Jakobwitz and Vincent Egan say Machiavellianism is an interpersonal strategy that is based upon self-interest, deception, and manipulation. Those who operate on the basis of a high-level of Machiavellianism practice deceit, flattery, and emotional detachment to manipulate others. They are likely to exploit others and are less likely to be concerned about other people, except as it affects their own self-interest. These are the kinds of people that may do anything to get what they want.

Jakobwitz and Egan noted that narcissism is related to a pathological form of self-love. The leader who chooses to hold on to this personality-driving monster has a sense of behavioral grandiosity, believes they are entitled, privileged and exempt. They think they are the exception to every rule, social convention, or law. The narcissist can be persistent in seeking attention, is extremely vain, excessively self-focused, and exploitative in interpersonal relationships. This kind of person needs to be told how good and successful they are even when they are not.

A person exhibiting psychopathic behaviors is selfish, callous, has superficial charm, and is remorselessness (cold and emotionally void), according to Jakobwitz and Egan. Psychopaths are skilled liars and, coupled with their shallow charisma, often manipulate and exploit others. They do not feel remorseful or guilty after deceiving or manipulating others. These are the kind of personalities that fill our prisons and mental hospitals, although there are plenty of them still on the loose.

Again, the above information is not an entire list of possible beliefs and behaviors but should serve as a good foundation for your further personal research.

You probably noticed that some of the behavioral traits apply to you. You are not alone. Most people have exhibited some of these traits sometime in their lifetime. Or to some low degree, people, in general, may exhibit Machiavellian, narcissistic, or psychopathic traits. They need not be a problem in most cases. They are a part of the human condition. However, significant issues may arise when these behaviors are dominating your life to a high degree.

You should not be feeding, strengthening, or operating out of that element of unregenerate, ungodly, unpurified, and rebellious anti-God nature that resides in some measure within us all. A leader, especially a Christian leader, should not be seeking power to feed or justify these behaviors. Remember who you are in Christ and who you represent. You are not your own because you were bought with a price (1 Corinthians 6:19–20). Operating as a CEO with these behaviors in the twenty-first century may be tolerated in corporate America, but not in God's kingdom.

WHAT IS YOUR TRIGGER?

According to American Addiction Centers, triggers are events or circumstances that produce an uncomfortable emotional or psychiatric symptom, such as anxiety, panic, discouragement, despair, or negative self-talk.

Triggers can be myriad and differ from person to person. In our context, you need to know your triggers (including situations, circumstances, and moments you feel vulnerable) that add fuel to your dark side.

What agitates you like nothing else? You need to know your propensities, predispositions, and personality type. If you don't know your triggers, you will not know what to stay away from or what aspects of your personality to work on. If ignited, you are reacting to your trigger rather than responding to the person or situation as you should. Knowing your triggers makes you a better leader.

Do certain smells, sights, and sounds cause you to flashback and relive the pain of previous moments? Thought triggers and the occurrences they set in motion may go far beyond the scope of leadership, and you need to know what they are.

Are there things that can happen in an instant that prompt you to react according to the flesh and not the Spirit? What generates an irrational response? Is it being touched in a certain way, certain kinds of family problems, financial hardships, feelings of loneliness, being overwhelmed, confused, or intimidated? Any of these things may cause sharp contrasts in behavior.

When you are aware of the things that cause you pain, you are able to better navigate through life by mitigating circumstances and seeking assistance, especially when leadership decisions need to be made.

HOW TO LEAD YOURSELF

Some Christian leaders will be uncomfortable when it comes to the concept of self-leadership. After all, on the face of it, attention to self seems narcissistic. But self-leadership is different because it puts the focus on the leader only to the degree that it empowers the leader to help others.

What are some practical things that you can do to influence yourself and so you can lead others? Here are three things that you can implement now.

Listen to what you say within the confines of your own mind. Your actions are dictated by your thoughts. Those who exercise self-leadership are constantly monitoring their self-talk. If it is negative, then they must exercise the discipline to convert it into positive self-talk. Positive self-talk is the launchpad for positive relationships and positive actions.

As Christian leaders, we have one of the most powerful resources in the universe, and that is the ability to talk to God in prayer. When self-talk fails us, then we can always go to God to receive direction. Prayer has the power to clear our sometimes confused minds and give us a clear leadership path. You exercise self-leadership when you monitor the words that are flowing through your mind and the content of your prayers.

Be willing to relinquish control. Narcissistic people are often control freaks. They believe that everything depends upon them, or at least that others follow their precise orders. Those who understand self-leadership abandon the need for control. Even Jesus on the cross knew when it was time to give control back to His heavenly Father. He said, "Father, into your hands I commit my spirit" (Luke 23:46).

A person who exercises self-leadership knows the boundaries of what he or she can and cannot control. Christian leaders must learn to discern what they can change and change it, but also when to stand back and let events unfold. It takes a certain kind of bravery to see situations unfold in ways that may seem undesirable to us as hands-on leaders, but we are called to know when God is at work and to give Him and other people the time and space to work His perfect will.

In my view, one of the greatest pitfalls of relinquishing control is the half-measure when a Christian leader gives control to God but continues to worry and be stressed about the situation. Worry is a narcissistic act when we fret about how the outcome will affect us. At the very least, worry is negative talk that never reaches God and only seeks to fuel the dark thoughts from our darker side.

Be Transparent. Narcissistic leaders are often entangled in a web of secrets, and we see that characteristic in political, military, and corporate leaders. Christian leaders need to escape this human tendency and be transparent.

What is transparency? It is first a state of mind that puts all people on a level footing. Groups or classes of people are not excluded from goal-setting or problem-resolution. All the stakeholders have a right to input their ideas and opinions. Leaders must have this sense of openness and not think that some must be excluded from involvement "for their own good."

Transparency encourages free and open exchange, and that may seem like a threat to some leaders. Yes, there is a time to be less transparent when it comes to counseling and related private communications, but privacy and transparency are different issues.

Second, transparency is a method to accomplish goals. There are no hidden agendas. Information is freely available for collaboration and collective decision-making. Christian leaders should be secure enough to encourage this type of transparency.

A Christian leader must have a strategy for breaking free conventional leadership modalities. These steps will help you rethink what you need to do to take care of yourself so that you can lead others.

7

Leadership Dark Sides

All people are flawed. Circumstances and experiences have a life-defining effect in both positive and negative ways. They affect the way we feel and act, our perceptions, and they affect leadership and leadership styles.

In 1887 Lord Acton wrote a letter to Church of England Archbishop Mandell Creighton. In it he said:

> Power tends to corrupt, and absolute power corrupts absolutely. Great men are almost always bad men, even when they exercise influence and not authority: still more when you superadd the tendency or the certainty of corruption by authority. There is no worse heresy than that the office sanctifies the holder of it. That is the point at which the end learns to justify the means.

His views had merit not only to the history of nations but also to our own personal life histories.

According to McIntosh and Rima, experiences and influences from childhood combined with the primal raw materials present in each of us develop our dark side. Unmet needs, coupled with the drive to achieve channeled in the wrong way, can derail a person's life. What motivates you can also destroy you. The need for balanced analysis (including reflection) is key. Situations resulting in unhealed pain or unmet needs can manifest itself in negative ways. The authors believe a leader can end up acting in compulsive, narcissistic, paranoid, codependent, or passive-aggressive ways.

THE COMPULSIVE LEADER

The leader with compulsive issues needs to maintain absolute order stemming from an obsessive personality. Work is often personalized and seen as a reflection of his or her personal performance. Perfection is their goal and is tied to a rigid lifestyle that is highly controlled and ordered. Compulsive leaders mask obsessive tendencies in the over-balanced pursuit of excellence, which is really obsessive perfectionism.

The two are not the same. Excellence is about the desire to improve continually. The obsessive person is driven by deep needs for acceptance. The person with obsessive-compulsive personality goal is to maintain control through meticulous attention to details, procedures, lists, or forms. These leaders manage every aspect of the organization, resist the need to delegate, and impose their input into everything.

A NARCISSISTIC LEADER

Narcissism is a part of the dark triad. The ambitions, judgments, and decisions of narcissistic leaders are motivated by unyielding egotism and self-absorption.

Leaders with this character flaw have a grand sense of self-importance and fixated with illusions of unlimited success or power. They believe they are above others, so they exploit them for personal gain, show little empathy, are envious, and demonstrate arrogant attitudes or behaviors. Narcissists may intentionally seek out positions of leadership to feed, promote, or satisfy their never-ending need for self-aggrandizement.

PARANOID LEADER

Paranoid leaders are led by fear. These leaders are suspicious and distrust others. They are often apprehensive and hostile. They are guarded in their relationships because they are fearful of potential rebellions.

Because of their mind-set, paranoid leaders often misinterpret words and actions. They infer unintended meaning as a pre-emptive strike against imagined attacks. They often micromanage others to preserve control over their irrational fears of imagined outcomes. They struggle in close relationships because they are afraid others will use personal information against them to undermine their headship. It is impossible for them to be open and vulnerable.

CODEPENDENT LEADER

Codependent leaders are more reactors then leaders. They fail to initiate action for fear of confrontation and will actively avoid it. Codependents take responsibility for the actions of others while blaming themselves. Leaders like this worry obsessively about the feelings of people. They tend to be repressed and frustrated and have difficulty giving honest expression to emotions or problems.

Being a codependent may be especially hard for spiritual leaders. They cannot confront the unbiblical behaviors of others. They often cover up problems under the false guise of being a peacemaker. The real issues are not dealt with, and that creates physical and moral distress.

PASSIVE-AGGRESSIVE LEADER

A passive-aggressive leader wants to appear to be cool, calm, and collected (passive), but is a boiling cauldron of aggressive anger just under the surface. There are numerous tendencies that affect this type of leader.

The passive-aggressive leader struggles with demands to satisfactorily perform tasks. Oddly enough, the primary indicator of a passive-aggressive leader is that they are habitually late. Lateness is an excuse to dictate and control situations in their favor. They also seek control by procrastination, stubbornness, being scatter-brained, and by being inefficient.

These leaders live in a cyclic pattern of fear. The obvious fear of failure and the not-so-common fear of success may lead to higher expectations with the possibility of failure. This kind of leader is inclined to emotional outbursts, such as anger, sadness, and irritation.

THE BENEFITS OF SELF-ANALYSIS

Leaders must evaluate themselves to identify and understand their strengths and weaknesses. Leaders cannot allow their flaws to damage their personal life or leadership role due to willful ignorance. Not taking a holistic stock of intrinsic gifts, propensities, proclivities, and flaws is unwise and needlessly risky.

Self-esteem is the starting point. Stanislava Popov, Miklos Biro, and Jelena Radanovic wrote in their paper, "Self-evaluation, and Mental Health: An Experimental Assessment," that self-esteem dictates self-worth because it represents how people feel about themselves, which affects their interaction with others at home and in the workplace. Self-evaluation illuminates an individual's persona so that improvement becomes possible.

EVALUATION TOOLS

Here are some simple inventories that leaders can take to get an inner perspective on their skillsets. The tools listed are far from an exhaustive list but serve as examples. Many tests are free and can be easily found online.

DELLAVECCHIO SPIRITUAL GIFTS INVENTORY

This survey is a tool to help place personnel in positions that are best suited to their innate God-given gifts. It can help people learn more about themselves by categorizing areas that match their capabilities and interests.

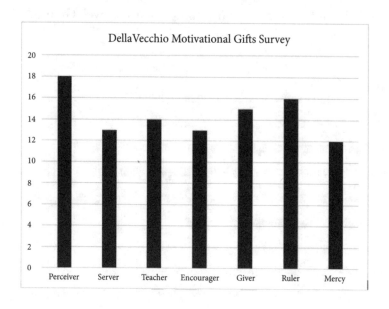

This inventory helps people understand where they may feel most comfortable, capable, and content. This test evaluates seven areas: perceiver, server, teacher, encourager, giver, ruler, and mercy.

CHRISTIAN CHARACTER SCORE

The Christian Character Score reflects the areas of compassion, forgiveness, gratitude, faithfulness, kindness, patience, joy, and love. The maximum score anyone can get is 90 since there is always room for improvement for those seeking Christlikeness. Each category is self-explanatory. The love score is an average of the other seven sections.

The example below reveals this person's Christian character needs much improvement. The lowest area, joy, accounts for how the person is enjoying their overall life. Patience addresses how the person handles circumstances. Kindness is more about what one does for others. Faithfulness reflects how an individual lives for God on a comprehensive level. Gratitude is about how content a person is in life.

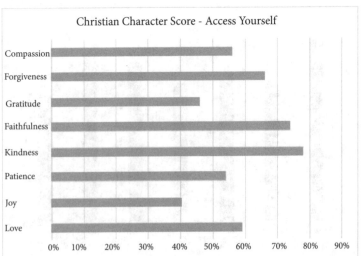

Christian Character Score - Access Yourself

Forgiveness is not just about simple forgiveness but also addresses the larger area of reconciliation. Finally, compassion is about touching the poor and needy. Of all the scores reflected, the most important score is the love score.

If a person garners a relatively low score, Assess Yourself, the organization that hosts the online survey, believes a person needs to make a significant readjustment in his or her life to put God first in all things. This person also needs to make prayer a regular practice and get an accountability partner who will lovingly help him or her to surrender fully to God.

NERIS ANALYTICS PERSONALITY INVENTORY

The inventory is used to identify a person's traits. A trait-based approach makes it simpler to measure parallels between personality traits and other characteristics. It spans sixteen personalities and even suggests the strengths and weaknesses of each person taking it. The example below illustrates the results of a low-level introvert, sensing, thinking, and judging individual.

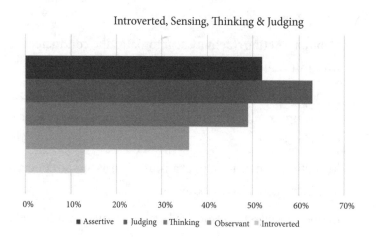

Introverted, Sensing, Thinking & Judging

■ Assertive ■ Judging ■ Thinking ■ Observant ■ Introverted

The Neris test is also based on the big five personality traits. The big five are openness, conscientiousness, extroversion, agreeableness, and neuroticism. To reiterate, there are numerous free inventories that can be found online. Take several to compare and contrast results.

PUTTING IT TOGETHER WITH REFLECTIVE LEADERSHIP

"How can I put these things together so I get a better picture of myself?" That may be the question you're asking yourself after you read about the dark triad and evaluation tools. One way is by instituting reflective leadership. According to author Makoto Matsuo, who wrote *Reflective Leadership and Team Learning: an Exploratory Study,* reflection refers to the practice of periodically stepping back to think about the meaning of what has transpired in the lives of individuals in an environment.

Matsuo noted that there are four levels of reflection classified into hierarchical levels:

- Habitual Action (activities automatically conducted or with minimum thought)
- Understanding (comprehending a concept without reflecting on its importance in personal or practical situations)
- Reflection (intentionally examining an issue of concern that is triggered by an experience)
- Intensive Reflection (higher-level reflective thinking that can result in changed thinking and behavior)

Being reflective can be transformative. Patricia Castelli, in her paper, "Reflective Leadership Review: A Framework for Improving Organizational Performance," noted that reflective leadership is about routinely dedicating time to practice reflection, which involves being aware of personal behaviors, situations and consequences all with the goal of improving performance. It can change behavior and actions when people take the reflective process seriously.

Be deliberate about thinking about yourself. If you react to a situation in the wrong way, think about why did you do it? Get to know the "whys" of your behavior. Why did you succeed in certain things? Why did you allow yourself to succumb to a moral failure? Why do certain words or phrases infuriate you? Why are there certain repeated cycles (patterns) in your life about money, relationships, character issues, or any other constant concerns you deal with?

Again, get to know you and your makeup or frame. Being contemplative helps leaders make sense of unclear, odd, or conflicted situations. Being introspective and thoughtful can also bring clarity to values, personal identity, emotions, motives, and goals. Also, it can lead to enhanced leadership behavior with respect to improved thinking, enhanced information collection, and goal setting.

HOW TO IMPLEMENT REFLECTIVE LEADERSHIP

Castelli explains the framework leaders need to construct for reflective leadership to flourish organizationally. It has six components:

- Create a Safe Environment. This is fostered by leaders that serve as role models, intentionally build relationships, value opposing views, and show integrity.

- Value Open Communication. Leaders should be accessible, transparent, welcome criticism, and be active listeners.

- Explain How Each Position Supports the Mission. Each employee, associate, or volunteer should know how their job impacts the mission and feels valued in their role.

- Build Self-Image. Leaders should be building the self-esteem and confidence of others, providing trustworthy feedback and direction, and act as a mentor and coach.

- Esteem Different Cultures. For reflective leadership to shift from being personal to organizational, those in charge need to value the diversity of different customs and values and create adaptable policies and procedures.

- Challenge the Mind. Leaders do not always go with the status quo. They question beliefs, are open to alternatives, and are willing to change.

This six-part process yields motivated people and improved performance. Reflection should cause a person to examine the ideas and assumptions that shape their behavior, which leads to greater self-awareness. This kind of contemplation increases a leader's understanding of problems, and it stimulates critical thinking skills that result in meaningful solutions.

Many people use contemplation in small bursts, but do not consider it to be a significant part of their personal and leadership arsenal. Many only dedicate time to think about others or themselves on birthdays, anniversaries, or during the holidays. However, this skillset needs to go far beyond just thinking about themselves or people around times of gift-giving and the holiday season. The proactive pursuit of reflective thinking is a tool to progressively steer decisions personally and organizationally and to consistently self-evaluate one's motives and mind-sets.

Put time to think on the calendar. Scheduled contemplation time for a few hours once a month, and set aside a day for it each quarter.

8

Character Check

As Shakespeare wrote in *Twelfth Night*, "Some are born great, some achieve greatness, and some have greatness thrust upon them. Thy Fates open their hands. Let thy blood and spirit embrace them." Whether you like it or not, when you are called to be a leader by God, you are also signing up to be a role model. It may not be fair, but it's true.

In the *Leadership Awakening*, Doug Stringer wrote that whenever you accept a position of leadership or gain any public visibility, you have set yourself up to be a role model. People will see your lifestyle and character as a pattern to follow. We never cease playing the childhood game of "Follow the Leader."

Paul conveyed this spiritual principle to Timothy, his apprentice. Paul said, "You, however, have followed my teaching, my conduct, my aim in life, my faith, my patience, my love, my steadfastness" (2 Timothy 3:10). Paul was even so bold to tell the Church of Corinth that they should imitate (follow) him as he imitated Christ. That is strong, confident leadership (1 Corinthians 11:1).

We know from Paul's letters that he knew people were watching him and that his behavior was influencing others. Paul understood the principle of the glasshouse.

THE GLASSHOUSE

Almost everything a leader does is on display for people to see. Most leaders have few unevaluated moments. People see how you dress, talk, walk (literally and metaphorically), and how you respond or react to situations and circumstances.

Such visibility can drive your commitment to Christ or can possibly become a disqualifier. Every leader who takes up their specific call needs to ask themselves if they are genuinely committed to walking with God. It's a heart issue. Those that have a problem with this should reevaluate if they are, in fact, ready to answer the call to leadership. Leadership comes with a price to pay. Being seen and noticed is often part of the call. Simply put, God puts people on display.

That is no surprise to people who are familiar with Bible leaders. God told Abram, "I will make of you a great nation, and I will bless you and make your name (reputation, fame, memorial, and monument) great (to grow, become great or important, promote, make powerful) so that you will be a blessing" (Genesis 12:2). God is not playing games when He chooses people to represent Him.

God made His covenant with David, and visibility was part of the deal. "I have been with you wherever you went and have cut off all your enemies from before you. And I will make for you a great name (reputation, fame, memorial, and monument), like the name of the great ones of the earth" (2 Samuel 7:9).

God told Ananias to go and pray for the dangerous and infamous Saul, who would later be known as the apostle Paul. The Lord said, "Go, for he is a chosen instrument of mine to carry my name before the Gentiles and kings and the children of Israel" (Acts 9:15).

In his book, Stringer reminds us that the church needs heroes today. Every generation needs men and women others can look up to and emulate.

A significant point of balance here is that just because you live in a glasshouse, it does not mean you cannot engage in normal activities or enjoy things that God has provided in life. A godly leader seeks to please the Lord, not people.

A Christian leader should always strive to be "close and clean"—close to God through spiritual disciplines and clean through a godly thought life. People look for godly and healthy role models, and they should be able to find one in you.

QUALIFY FROM THE INSIDE OUT

It can be almost comical to compare the way God selects someone for leadership verses the way corporate America does it. The world's view is starkly different from the biblical worldview. In corporate America, hiring officials tend to prioritize a candidate's education and experience. In the kingdom of God, character is all-important. It is as if God is continually asking the question, "Can I trust you?"

We see this in Titus 1:6–9 where Paul listed the desired characteristics of leaders:

> If anyone is above reproach, the husband of one wife, and his children are believers and not open to the charge of debauchery or insubordination. For an overseer, as God's steward, must be above reproach.

He must not be arrogant or quick-tempered or a drunkard or violent or greedy for gain, but hospitable, a lover of good, self-controlled, upright, holy, and disciplined. He must hold firm to the trustworthy word as taught, so that he may be able to give instruction in sound doctrine and also to rebuke those who contradict it.

Paul knew the growing church's progressive success would need to be in the hands of faithful men who would win souls, teach, and demonstrate godly leadership. Titus was in Crete to select leaders who exhibited this level of maturity or character.

It's significant to note that character trumps things, such as looks, position, or wealth. Paul addressed character before heretical teachings and the need for sound doctrine. He understood that the right leadership in place was needed to sustain and grow the organization. Titus is given the responsibility to appoint elders (leaders) to oversee the people and administration of the church.

Titus 1:6–9 is the prerequisite checklist. The idea is to use it to find leaders who are already leading, in spiritual and practical ways, in their own sphere of influence. These qualifications have a direct tie to a person's godly character.

Leaders are qualified by their established observed consistent behavior. That means leadership is more than just about mental and technical knowledge. It is about character, values, virtues, and standards.

A key point here is that people aspiring to assume a leadership role and who do not exhibit these attributes are already disqualified. They are disqualified by God. Leaders need to stop looking at candidates' resumes merely for experience and education and look deeper for strong character traits.

In his book, Stringer explains that from the moment a Christian accepts a position of influence, their life is not their own. He also says that for every new level of promotion or visibility, there must be a new level of surrender (humility, consecration, accountability, and intercession). All of God's leaders must align themselves in attitude and actions with the character of Jesus.

While many point to the outward sides of a person (looks, pedigree, education, track record, etc.), God is looking at the heart (1 Samuel 16:7). For those called to lead, their alignment to God's ways brings His quality stamp approval. This approval often leads to God's precious anointing. Character is the container for the anointing of God.

By scriptural standards, practically everything that qualifies a person for leadership is related to character. We see the spiritual meet the practical in 1 Timothy 3:1–13, which is the job description for leaders known as overseers and deacons.

> The saying is trustworthy: If anyone aspires to the office of overseer, he desires a noble task. Therefore an overseer must be above reproach, the husband of one wife, sober-minded, self-controlled, respectable, hospitable, able to teach, not a drunkard, not violent but gentle, not quarrelsome, not a lover of money. He must manage his own household well, with all dignity keeping his children submissive, for if someone does not know how to manage his own household, how will he care for God's church? He must not be a recent convert, or he may become puffed up with conceit and fall into the condemnation of the devil. Moreover, he must be well thought of by outsiders, so that he may not fall into disgrace, into a snare of the devil.

Deacons likewise must be dignified, not double-tongued, not addicted to much wine, not greedy for dishonest gain. They must hold the mystery of the faith with a clear conscience. And let them also be tested first; then let them serve as deacons if they prove themselves blameless. Their wives likewise must be dignified, not slanderers, but sober-minded, faithful in all things. Let deacons each be the husband of one wife, managing their children and their own households well. For those who serve well as deacons gain a good standing for themselves and also great confidence in the faith that is in Christ Jesus.

Paul's instruction to Timothy about how to select leaders is directly related to a person's character. One that is under control, disciplined, and has a lifestyle conducive to the fruit of the Spirit.

Being perfect is impossible and a myth, but every Christian leader must have mature character and integrity before God and men. Christian leaders do not lead with words but with integrity. In *Be Light*, Samuel Rodriquez wrote that Christians must unify themselves. This unity is comprised of the heart, mind, and entire being. It is about pouring mercy to others, bringing grace to those in need, and self-denial. No matter what, your will must be involved. God does not require you to be perfect, but you must be willing and obedient.

Dr. Robert Clinton wrote in his book, *The Making of a Leader*, that there are many ways to measure success in ministry. He says the primary way is by what God does to and in the leader, not through him. That means we need to stop looking at productivity, activities, and achievements as the standard.

The gifts of the Spirit and the fruit of the Spirit go hand-in-hand. In balance, they signify a mature Christian. God wants to first work "in you" (Colossians 1:27) and then "through you."

GUARD YOUR HEART

The book of Proverbs is filled with nuggets of wisdom. Proverbs 4:23 says, "Keep your heart with all vigilance, for from it flow the springs of life." Dr. Clinton noted that apart from character, ministry is only a religious activity or religious business. But the church is not corporate America. We must guard against it being that. Again, this proverb scripture refers to the hearts of people. This means the mind, conscience, moral character, seat of appetites, emotions, and character.

What is in your heart impacts, influences, and acts as a border for your life. Remember, the best way to lead is from the inside out. Your job as a Christian leader is to keep a pure heart. That is not always easy, but this is the reason why spiritual discipline is mandatory for Christian leaders.

How proactive are you when it comes to maintaining a pure heart?

9

Boundaries

If you ever saw the US Air Force Air Demonstration Squadron in action, a group known as the Thunderbirds, you have probably never forgotten them. They started in 1953 with early F-84G jet fighters, and have upgraded over the years to the sleek, fast jets that inspire us all.

The pilots are supported by approximately 120 maintenance and support personnel. They travel around the world putting on amazing aerial demonstrations for multitudes.

Most who watch them are astounded by the beautiful planes and the roar of their engines, but the most remarkable part of their display is their close formation flying. In their diamond configuration, the aircraft may be only a few feet from each other as they maneuver at high speed.

You probably think the Thunderbirds pilots get special training to be able to fly so close with such precision. True. Depending on the specific aircraft, Air Force fighter pilots are often trained to do some close formation flying. However, Thunderbirds pilots get extra training to enhance their disciplined, synchronized aerobatic skills and are building on abilities they already have.

Wonder how Thunderbirds pilots manage to maintain control that makes the difference between the high-speed harmony of their show and an inflight collision? What makes the difference between a synchronized flight and an aerial disaster? They use a technique called "station-keeping." They keep their focus on certain predetermined features of the planes around them, in relation to their own plane, and thus have a reference for judging distance. Simply put, they need to know the boundaries.

Boundaries are important to people on personal and organizational levels. If individuals are not continually "station-keeping," they will collide with the people closest to them.

Since leadership is a social enterprise, leaders must be knowledgeable about boundaries to ensure there is no abuse of power, overreach of authority, or social breach that can lead to an inappropriate relationship of any type. Boundaries promote positive social interaction.

WHAT ARE THE BOUNDARIES?

A boundary is a line that defines territory. According to Proverbs 4:23, boundaries are the gatekeepers of the soul. Boundaries are guiding principles, rules, or limits a person creates to identify the reasonable, safe, and acceptable ways to behave, and how the person will respond when someone steps outside those limits.

In their book *Boundaries*, Dr. Henry Cloud and Dr. John Townsend say that a boundary shows you where a person ends and where someone else begins. It is all about who owns or is responsible for a particular space. It is about personal protection from being harmed, like a thick sheet of glass or a high unclimbable gate at the zoo that separates you from the animals. The authors define seven broad boundary spheres:

- Behavioral—Behaviors have consequences
- Spiritual—A decision to have personal beliefs and experiences with God
- Material—The limits you set about lending money and your possessions, such as cars, tools, food, clothes, books, or other personal items
- Physical—Who, how, where, and when someone can touch you
- Mental—Thoughts, values, opinions, beliefs, attitudes, where you guard against manipulation or intimidation
- Emotional—Know your feelings and responsibilities to yourself and other people in regard to expressing them
- Sexual—Comfort level with sexual touch and activity; who, what, where, and when

It's important to remember that boundaries go both ways. People should accept your restrictions just as you respect their boundaries. Setting and honoring boundaries is about mutual respect. The restrictions dictate what is allowed in our personal territory and what is not allowed.

A PEOPLE OF BOUNDARIES

The guardian mind-set leaders establish for their personal lives should also carry over to their professional or ministerial role. Plainly speaking, leaders need to set boundaries for themselves and model them for the people they lead. In his book, *Boundaries for Leaders,* Dr. Henry Cloud said that successful leaders define limits in these areas:

- The vision, focus, and attention to activities that create organizational forward movement
- The *esprit de corps,* morale or the emotional climate of the organization and its culture
- The unity of the organization
- The thinking and beliefs of the organization
- Team performance and development
- Self-leadership, self-control to maintain established values

In short, leaders with boundaries make sure certain things happen while preventing others, and keep the organization moving forward toward predetermined organizational goals.

Those in charge are guardians of beliefs. God-ordained leaders act as traffic police who constantly direct others to the mission and vision of the church or organization. They allow some traffic through while other traffic is stopped.

BOUNDARIES AS AN ANTIDOTE TO MISSION CREEP

The power of focus is always in the leader's hands, and they are charged with the responsibility to guard their institutions against mission creep.

Mission creep is when an organization is constantly expanding its mission beyond original objectives. For example, consider a group founded to combat human trafficking in Europe. After a few years of success, the leadership decides to take up missionary work in Northern Africa. Then after a short time, the mission expands to fighting against diseases such as cholera and malaria in third-world nations. After even more time passes, the leadership decides to take up the fight against political corruption. The mission creep is that the mission was initially to combat human trafficking but expanded to missionary work, medical assistance, and then battling political corruption.

There is nothing inherently wrong with expanding the mission of the organization. However, it must be accomplished strategically. The CEO and or executive team can decide to do whatever is desired and agreed upon by the necessary stakeholders. The problems come when there is a lack of organizational focus combined with limited resources, such as finances, people, or time.

The same can be said of local church organizations. The initial goal is often to win souls for Christ and make disciples in their local area, but mission creep develops into the church putting their limited resources into activities like:

- Choir competitions
- Church athletic teams
- A food pantry
- A prison outreach
- Sending missionary teams overseas
- Caring for the sick
- Sheltering the homeless
- Clothing the needy
- Leading education reform in schools
- Fighting social issues, such as racial injustices

All these things are good and even necessary. The church should have inroads into the community and society in general to effect change and be the salt and light that Christ desires.

The problem is when faith-based organizations, ministries, and churches do things that God never really ordained for them to do. Often in these mission creep situations, people eventually burn out. They try to do too much with too few resources. Take a typical electrical outlet in a house or apartment. The one outlet is not meant to run the washing machine, dryer, dishwasher, TV, HVAC, iron, and every lighting fixture in the place and at the same time. Overload results in a shutdown.

Leaders must be gatekeepers who stop what needs to stop and let pass what should pass. They set boundaries and limits. Leaders should only champion what they have been called, anointed, or received God's grace to do. God often calls people to a thing or several things but not all things.

Dr. Cloud says that leaders set boundaries for what gets attention among the many distractions that are bound to materialize. He says leaders ensure that followers are doing the most important thing at the most strategic time. They prevent people from accomplishing what is not important, unnecessary, or destructive.

THE SPIRITUAL PRINCIPLE

Acts 6:1-4 demonstrates this principle. One group of Christians became concerned because their people were not getting enough food. The Twelve had a meeting with other disciples and said, "It is not right that we should give up preaching the word of God to serve tables." So, the Christian community selected "seven men of good repute, full of the

Spirit and of wisdom" to wait tables and freed the Twelve to devote themselves to prayer and to the ministry of the word.

The Twelve saw a boundary was required. They decided that there were some things that they should be doing and some things that they should not be doing. Others took on the responsibility for another set boundary, which focused on an equitable distribution of resources.

Today's leaders need to define which areas of responsibility they need to embrace and which ones they should reject and delegate to others.

ASKING "WHY?"

Why? One of the best questions a person can ask. John Manning, who wrote *The Disciplined Leader,* noted that the disciplined leader has high regard for the question "Why?" The question can be a catalyst for positive change, drive performance, develop people, and bolster an organization's level of excellence. "Why" can be a catalyst for a leader to look below the surface of an issue and get to the core of it. An honest answer to "Why" can reveal which objective is the right fit for an organization's mission.

For spiritual leaders, in particular, a good idea is not necessarily a God idea. Just because you can do something does not mean you should do it. The question of "Why are we doing this?" can press people past shallow mental barriers and assumptions. The "Why" question can yield insights into struggles and their solutions. Healthy organizations question the conventional mind-set so they can grow.

It's always important to ask the right questions. Why are employees missing goals? Why am I saying this? Why is the organization taking this new initiative? Why not? Leaders ask and keep asking, "Why?" The "Why" question always leads to the core of intentionality. Is the intention congruent with the mission?

For example, there is a faith-based organization whose mission is to:

- Turn Hearts
- Develop People for Christ
- Advance God's Kingdom

That ideology is working its way throughout the entire organization. Every department is aligning itself with that mission. Even the comptroller knows they are charged to track and report the financial status of the organization in accordance with the "turn, develop, and advance" mission. They know the "Why" behind what they do. This applies to all workgroups. The goal is for everyone to know the "Why" of what they are doing.

MAPPING YOUR BOUNDARIES

Leaders need to draw two maps. One is a map of what they consider to be their personal territory. How far will you go before you cross the line? It is a helpful exercise to draw an imaginary map and show your personal, family, and work boundaries.

Then, in collaboration with others, mark the boundaries for your organization. Will you be able to address core needs within those boundaries, or will you always feel compelled by others to expand your territory?

You can only expand so far as an individual or an organization. When you have a map on your wall, it is easy for you and others to visualize your boundaries and keep within them.

10

Leadership Development

The path to becoming a United States Navy SEAL is an arduous one. SEALs have a unique position in our military. Much of their work is clandestine as they deter threats, but that type of activity enables the government to risk less military lives than if other actions were used. Rather than send in a large force, a few men are able to achieve a military objective by stealth.

The thing that interests me about SEALs is how they are selected. There are many steps required to become a member of this elite fighting force. There are several paths to becoming a SEAL, but all start by joining the Navy, going to basic training, and expressing an interest in the Special Operations division.

Once you prove to be physically fit and have the mental alacrity for the job, a SEAL recruit receives Basic Underwater Demolition training. When you meet the minimum requirements there, you move on to different phases, which include more physical training, learning to dive, and land warfare skills.

You would think that would be all the training a SEAL would need. However, only after all that is a candidate allowed to attend SEAL Qualification Training (SQT). After successful completion of SQT, the candidate becomes a full-fledged SEAL team member.

Why have I explained this rigorous process? It is to point out development, even leadership development, starts in the heart and the mind of the individual. A SEAL is not selected randomly from a group. Initial selection for the program is made by the candidate. The candidate must have a strong desire to join and have the stamina to continue.

The performance of the candidate is carefully observed. If the candidate is building a strong body, has a sharp mind, and learns the skills, then no barrier is placed in his way. If the candidate fails in any of these ways, he disqualifies himself.

The whole point seems to be that if you can survive the training, then you can accomplish the missions given to you.

When we think about selecting and developing Christian leaders, we want to select and encourage those who have already demonstrated their desire and determination, without any advanced promise they will be picked to lead in top positions.

Leaders need to develop leaders. *In The Making of a Leader,* Dr. J. Robert Clinton wrote that a major responsibility of all leadership is to select rising leaders. Leaders must continually be mindful of this and see it as a core focus. The success of any organization rests on the leadership, whether stated in a job description or not. Leadership development is not a side task or caveat to a leader's responsibility but should be a high-ranking priority.

Those vested with the responsibility to lead departments and people should be observing those God is selecting and processing, and find ways to enhance their development.

The main function of the Body of Christ is to develop leaders. In the book, *Designed to Lead,* written by Eric Geiger and Kevin Peck, the authors note that the church is uniquely set apart to develop leaders whose purpose is to advance the gospel. As Paul told Timothy, "What you have heard from me in the presence of many witnesses entrust to faithful men, who will be able to teach others also" (2 Timothy 2:2). This is leadership development. Jesus gives us the purpose of this development: "Go therefore and make disciples of all nations, baptizing them in the name of the Father and of the Son and of the Holy Spirit" (Matthew 28:19).

Geiger and Peck remind us that this Great Commission is God's operational strategy and that God's process is discipleship. Discipleship is developing believers to grow in Christ over time. God has designed the church (His people) to influence others by the power of the Spirit.

This is all encapsulated in Ephesians 4:11–13 where Paul said, "And he gave the apostles, the prophets, the evangelists, the shepherds and teachers, to equip the saints for the work of ministry, for building up the Body of Christ, until we all attain to the unity of the faith and of the knowledge of the Son of God, to mature manhood, to the measure of the stature of the fullness of Christ."

LEADERSHIP DEVELOPMENT IN BIBLICAL PERSPECTIVE

Specified leaders are to build up and mature others. The books of Timothy and Titus also reflect on how Paul taught and developed these men as leaders to lead the church.

Notice how the hand of God steers people to their divine destinies. Consider Moses, who was trained in the house of

Pharaoh before he ran off and eventually became a shepherd. The teachings that Moses received in the house of Pharaoh, and his later shepherding duties were the training grounds for his life development. That training would later prove advantageous in the hands of God as Moses led the children of Israel from captivity to freedom.

Think about David. He was anointed to be king as a young boy and later lived in the palace to serve King Saul. Although innocent of wrongdoing, Saul eventually came to despise David and wanted to dispose of him. David ran for his life. All the while, David was learning things, such as military operations, honor, and the journey of trusting God, all of which was useful when David became king.

Joseph's life was also filled with circumstances that were part of his leadership development. Joseph was almost murdered by his brothers, and they sold him into slavery. Joseph would later be wrongfully imprisoned for years. Eventually, God used Joseph to minister to the king and became one of the most powerful men in the land. God chose to develop Joseph through time and various painful events in his life.

An apprenticeship in the work of obeying God is a time-honored method of leadership development. However, organizational leadership development programs need not be as long, traumatic, and dramatic as some of the aforementioned life experiences, but they do illustrate one of God's ways of development. God wants all leaders to grow. All have gifts, but those need to be developed too. We all learn by watching and helping skilled people do their work and through the personal challenges we face.

LEADERSHIP DEVELOPMENT VIA ORGANIZATIONAL CULTURE

Culture is one of the main things that leaders can implement as a controlling force in their organization, whether they are physically present or not. In fact, not paying attention to culture could unknowingly derail an organizational leader's best efforts.

Leaders need to understand the culture to establish a holistic leadership development program. To have leadership development become a part of the organization, leaders must recognize that it's central to an organization's strategy, not something subordinate to it.

ORGANIZATIONAL CULTURE

As initially noted in chapter two - Edgar Schein defined culture as a pattern of shared beliefs (whether known or unknown) and learned behavior that is considered appropriate and consequently taught to others. As a worker, there is no way around it. The culture of an organization is all-encompassing, incorporating the vision, values, norms, systems, symbols, language, assumptions, beliefs, and even organizational proclivities and habits.

By using culture as a designing tool, management can turn workers into a cohesive family. The underlying philosophy of business culture is multifaceted.

THE ARTIFACTS OF CULTURE

Culture is established, supported, and even changed, based on the basis of three levels. The first level has to deal with an organization's artifacts.

Artifacts are superficial and easily noticeable. Artifacts are organizational tangibles and intangibles such as the architecture and layout of the physical environment (open cubicles, closed office doors), language among employees, type of technology and products used, required workplace attire, a published list of organizational values, ritual ceremonies, and other things easily noticed.

THE CODE OF THE CULTURE

The second level of culture is leadership's espoused beliefs and values. Espoused values are those that the organizational leadership says they live and lead by. They are beliefs in theory but may not necessarily be practiced.

In laymen's terms, the old adages of "Talk is cheap" and "It's not what you say, but what you do" can be applied to add contextual meaning. An example of espoused values is an organization that says they are about community and neighborhood support but never does anything tangible for the community in terms of community service, fiscal support, acquiring local hires or local business development. Espoused values also represent the ideals, goals, aspirations, and beliefs of a group.

THE ASSUMPTIONS OF THE CULTURE

The third and deepest tier of culture in an organization are what Schein called underlying assumptions. These assumptions represent one's pattern of thinking and actually influence or dictate behavior.

They are determined behavior patterns, perceptions, and unconscious values. Beliefs like these are the hardest to change. They cause people to think, act, and behave in ways they may not know why.

LEADERSHIP DEVELOPMENT

What many must understand is that leadership is a process, not an event. It's the holistic approach that will make development a part of the company's culture. The strategic approach will be more effective.

Strategy, like leadership, is essentially a social process since it deals with people. The strategic plan for an organization can be defined in several ways. It is essentially about a firm's direction, vision, and tactics.

Leadership development needs to be tightly tied to a company's strategy for it to stick. That, in turn, becomes part of the organizational culture. According to the Center for Creative Leadership, there are three drivers of leadership development:

- Assessment

- Challenge

- Support

It is the tripod of leadership development for organizational stick-to-itiveness.

ASSESSMENT

Assessments can come in many forms. On the individual level, it simply means to evaluate a person's skills. It is about knowing where one's skills (strengths, weaknesses, levels of performance) are now and future developmental needs.

An assessment can also come in the form of feedback. Asking others such as peers, spouse, children, parents, customers, or supervisor about your performance can have an impact.

Assessments generally are questions listed and based on a set of required or desired organizational leadership competencies. It is about measuring an individual's skills needed for success.

The results may illustrate what skills need to be enhanced by training and used for developmental purposes. When was the last time your organization assessed its people to make sure those with the requisite gifts, talents, and callings were placed in the right jobs so both person and organization can flourish? An assessment helps put the right people in the right place on a continuing basis.

CHALLENGE

Leaders are often developed through experiences. Challenging times tend to be a proving ground for skills and temperament. The comfort zone is not a place where anyone is stretched to get better and forces no one to mature in skills and competencies, so challenges are like a stress test.

Challenges can provide a rich opportunity for leaders to understand better their capabilities and capacities to lead and change according to the need. To meet a challenge, one might experiment with their own theories to see if they really work. Challenges can be a variety of things: dealing with difficult people, increased responsibilities, new assignments, promotions, demotions, or almost anything else that breaks routine.

To meet the challenge, leaders need to forget preconceived ideas, disregard the typical way of doing things, and be willing to use available people and resources to provide answers to problems.

Challenges, conflicts, and experiments all amount to learning. The learning comes by taking the challenges head-on and doing the work required to overcome them. The pressures of leadership can come from within (internal or self-imposed pressure) or without (other people or situations). Observations can produce theories and philosophies, but overcoming a problem produces experienced leaders.

When was the last time you or anyone in your organization was challenged to stretch beyond their typical day-to-day, routine, and mundane limits? Is anyone truly being developed? Leaders get developed and develop others through challenges.

SUPPORT

In the *Handbook of Leadership Development* by Ellen Van Velsor, Cynthia McCauley, and Marian Ruderman, the authors say that organizations are most effective at developing leaders when they have the commitment and involvement of senior management. To be clear, just because organizational leaders support something does not mean it will succeed. But you can be sure that without leadership support, a company's leadership development initiatives will not be as successful as if it had the backing and full endorsement of the executive leadership.

Once the leadership body has bought into the notion of leadership development, it may prove easier to influence the support of others in the firm, such as associates, coworkers, family, coaches, and other external audiences.

Next, organizational procedures should be used to produce norms, rules, and systems that can be compiled to support the overall culture. Without the tie of the leadership and organizational procedures, the firm's culture could end up fighting leadership as opposed to being a positive and beneficial force. Some typical ways leadership support is exhibited is in mentoring, coaching, strategy formation, encouraging teamwork, and networking.

GETTING PERSPECTIVE

Although getting into the precise details of developing a leadership program is beyond the scope of this book, it is important to remember that the drivers of leadership development (assessment, challenge, and support) are needed no matter its purpose or how the organization is structured. Any program must adjust the larger organization's goals and structure.

For example, remember the previously discussed faith-based organization with the mission to turn, develop, and advance others? Well, the organization should recruit new hires according to those precepts. The standard people are evaluated against should be guided by that model. Promoting people should always be done to capture and fulfill the model. The limited resources of the organization need to align itself to that mission.

All organizations must take leadership development seriously. It must be inculcated into the organization's cognitive and practical operational decisions, just like the mission should be.

We must always keep in mind that leadership maturation is a process, not an event. It is process-driven, and that may lead to events, not the other way around. Leadership development is more than just a quarterly training or an item to mark off of a checklist. It must embody the overall values and goals of the organization.

SEEKING THOSE GOD HAS CHOSEN

Earlier I mentioned some of the great leaders of the Bible, such as Moses, Joseph, and David in the Old Testament, and Timothy and Titus in the New Testament. Most experienced long, dramatic experiences that prepared them to do the work of serving God in the face of conflict with the cultures of their time. Today, leadership training does not need to be as arduous, but there are some biblical aspects that remain important.

As leaders, we have an obligation to keep a sharp eye out for those leaders to carry the torch into the future. Here are some characteristics you can use to identify future Christian leaders. Candidates with these characteristics are the people in which we want to invest our own lives to train for Christian service.

A Call from God. People serve God for many reasons and for varying periods of time. We always want to encourage volunteer workers who do so much to further the cause of Christ. We are always thankful for such people. Yet, when we are talking about Christian leaders in this context, we are also talking about those who have a full-time vocational commitment. It is important that these people have a sense of calling from God.

We are all called to the followers of Christ (Luke 9:23), but a call to service is a very specific thing. Abraham had a specific calling (Genesis 12:1-9), as did the apostle Paul (Romans 1:1). Paul intimated that a sense of calling was essential to the offices of the church he describes in Ephesians 4:11–12.

There is testing involved when someone asserts they have a calling to service and leadership. It must be confirmed by others in the person's local Christian community. That confirmation should include validation of the fruits of the Spirit in the life of the person, as Paul describes in Galatians 5:22–23.

A zeal to serve God. Zeal is defined as "great energy or enthusiasm in pursuit of a cause or an objective." Sadly, this characteristic has been devalued in modern times. Society tends to brand a zealot as an undesirable person. Zealousness is often used in a pejorative way in reference to those who desire to serve God.

In his book, *Practical Religion*, J. C. Ryle put zeal in a proper perspective for us. He said: "A zealous person in Christianity is preeminently a person of one thing. It is not enough to say that they are earnest, strong, uncompromising, meticulous, wholehearted, and fervent in spirit. They only see one thing, they care for one thing, they live for one thing, they are swallowed up in one thing; that one thing is to please God."

We want to look for potential leaders with that kind of zeal.

A teachable spirit. No one should be a leader unless they are first a follower. They cannot be a teacher unless they are first a student. A teachable spirit is not about a person's knowledge, academic degrees, or age. It is about having a lifelong openness to ideas that enhance understanding and growth. The best leaders are always learning.

It is interesting that the Bible connects a teachable spirit with spiritual discipline. Proverbs 5:12–13 says, "How I hated discipline, and my heart despised reproof! I did not listen to the voice of my teachers or incline my ear to my instructors." The Apostle Paul advises Timothy to seek leaders who fulfill particular spiritual and practical requirements in 1 Timothy 3, and they include the characteristics of those who have a teachable spirit.

Spiritual gifts. It may seem odd that I place spiritual gifts as the fourth characteristic that we are seeking in potential leaders. There is confusion about spiritual gifts and clarity about them is important.

Paul identifies three different aspects that we tend to lump together as spiritual gifts. They are:

- Gifts to the church. These are really offices, such as apostles, prophets, evangelists, pastors, and teachers. (Ephesians 4:11).

- Empowerment Gifts. Certain people have a special gift to encourage others, show mercy, and otherwise build them up in the faith. Paul talks about these motivational or inspirational gifts in Romans 12:6–8.

- Ministry Gifts. These include wisdom, knowledge, faith, healing, miracles, administration, leadership, distinguishing spirits, and others. Paul writes about these gifts in 1 Corinthians 12:8–10, 27–31.

Yes, there is some overlap in these types of gifts. However, when we seek leaders to develop, we want to put the focus on their callings and their accompanying giftings.

A servant heart. Why are Christian leaders required to have a servant heart? Because Christian leaders should want to emulate the heart of Christ, who had the humility to wash the feet of His disciples (John 13:1–17). A servant heart is an attitude of caring and humility.

Jesus made servanthood a qualification for service. There was a time when James and John were involved in a power struggle with the other disciples. Jesus put that power in proper perspective. He said, "You know that those who are considered rulers of the Gentiles lord it over them, and their great ones exercise authority over them. But it shall not be so among you. But whoever would be great among you must be your servant" (Mark 10:42–43).

Our task is not recruiting leaders based on corporate criteria. It is discovering those whom God has already chosen. When we find them, we want to do everything possible to help them mature into the fullness of what the Lord wants them to be.

11

A Leadership Development Mind-set

Most are unaware of Pete Schoening. He was an American mountain climber who was atop 25,251 foot K2 in Kashmir in 1953 when a series of horrible events occurred.

A small group started toward the summit, but a storm arrived as they neared it, and they became trapped. One man suffered a deep venous thrombosis and collapsed. The others put him in a sleeping bag and began to haul him down the mountain to save his life.

Night came, the storm raged, and several of the men fell over the edge into the abyss. Fortunately, they were connected by a rope that was supported by a belay.

Schoening was in a position to act. Using heroic strength and skill, he wedged his axe against a boulder and stopped the fall, and then he singlehandedly saved the men by pulling them back onto the ledge. He was in the right place at the right time with the right attitude and skills to make a life-changing difference.

Like Schoening, who desired to climb K2, Christian leaders must take to the mountains for God. Our ultimate goal is to rescue the perishing. At the same time, we are developing others to climb their respective mountains.

More leaders need this mind-set. The impact of godly leadership must extend far beyond the four walls of the church building. For example, Johnny Enlow, in his book *The Seven Mountain Prophecy*, said the Lord raises up people and gives them the opportunity to fulfill the entire Great Commission to disciple nations and not just individuals.

EVERY FIELD IS A MISSION FIELD

The concern is the missional work of the church is not just overseas in other nations, but a mission field can be corporate America. Or any secular industry that influences society. In the book *The Executive Calling* by Roger Andersen, he tells of a study that was conducted among 2,000 people who attended church on a regular basis. They were asked if they ever heard a sermon that applied biblical principles to everyday work issues. More than 90 percent said no. This negative response should be surprising, shocking, and perhaps even offensive to God's people endowed with leadership ability and responsibility.

Leaders need to ask themselves the hard questions about their calling. What human or spiritual needs are they called to meet? What people group are they charged by the Lord to serve?

The mindset of some leaders is far too myopic. Most people who support faith-based organizations such as churches and other nonprofits (including many of the workers) are not going to be preachers, apostles, prophets, evangelists, pastors, teachers, and missionaries. They will be IT professionals, drivers, teachers, government employees, sales professionals, carpenters, military, policemen, firefighters, and a myriad of other vocations.

The point is, leaders must not create a façade that only those called to work in traditional churches and ministries have callings that matter. That is just not true. God calls us all to our vocations. There is no artificial separation between the sacred and the secular. We are a holy people (1 Peter 2:9), seeking to do God's will regardless of our station in life.

Andersen noted that the church has lost the respect of secular vocations. And that the church has allowed work and religion to be separate departments. From a Christian's perspective, a person's calling, gifting, vocation, ministry, and work is interrelated in God's divine order.

Christians must know that work is significant to God, and there is plenty in the Bible about being called to serve and to do something for God regardless of job title. Jesus surrounded Himself with fishermen, agricultural workers, soldiers, government officials, homeworkers, and those with other vocations, and the message was the same for all.

Vocation is deeply connected to a person's identity, as God's purpose for one's life is found in God's design of one's life. But one's calling is not always made apparent. Christians need to examine their lives for particularities to find out what they are created for. The created must seek the Creator. It is important for an individual to seek God's will for their life. Personal desire must be synchronized with God's ordained purpose. This idea should support an understanding among servant leaders that not everyone is supposed to be a local church leader, but God wants Christian leaders in all strata of society.

In 1942, Christian author Dorothy Sayers questioned how anyone could remain interested in a religion that is perceived to have no concern with one's work, something that makes up nine-tenths of their life? Andersen noted that today, work encompasses approximately 71 percent of a person's time.

Sayers said that Christians, and especially Christian clergy, must understand that when a person is called to a secular job, it is as true of a vocation as one called to religious work. Every worker is called to serve God is his or her profession, not outside of it. The underlying reality, often ignored, is that God is concerned with our work because it is such a dominant ingredient of our lives. Our work is the main way we occupy our life. And, above all, He cares about our lives.

Andersen believes commerce (which is supposed to be beneficial to all parties involved) is often perverted and polluted by godless or immoral executives. Hence, there is no reason for Christians to avoid leadership responsibilities in secular arenas. The Christian is supposed to be salt and light for a reason. Likewise, capitalism in and of itself is not bad or wrong, but it has often been abused by those in positions of power with low moral standards.

The God who is concerned about church leaders is also concerned about scientists, salespeople, mechanics, plumbers, and all other occupations. And yes, Christians in all occupations are charged to exercise Christ-inspired leadership regardless of their role.

SECTORS OF SOCIETY

Enlow wrote as the world becomes darker, the light of Christ shines brighter. Our present era is the church's opportunity to shine brighter and to manifest Christ's solutions for society. And this means shaping society beyond the confines of the church walls. The Lord wants His church to fulfill the Great Commission to disciple nations, not just individuals.

It is about ministering, leading and developing others to be Christlike in the marketplace. Consider your assigned place of work as a God-assigned mission. Enlow identifies seven areas (called mountains) of major influence in society and says that Christians need to be directly involved in each of them. Based on Revelation 5:1–12, they are:

- Media

- Government

- Education

- Economy (finance)

- Family

- Religion

- Celebration (arts and entertainment)

These areas represent culture-shaping spheres of power.

Enlow believes the world has an incorrect image of God as the church attempts humanistic solutions to society's problems. The older saints are dying, and the next generation is refusing to enter into a dead church. God's leaders need to understand that people who are interested in an authentic move of God (experiencing His presence and power) are often offered mere entertainment to satisfy them, and they are rejecting it. They want meat, not a plant-based substitute that is meat flavored. Servant leaders need to become cognizant of the fact that humanistic solutions to spiritual issues are not solutions at all.

To reiterate, Christian leaders are not just to prepare others for life within the walls of the church but must have a broader mandate to teach, train, and equip others to act like Jesus in every sector of society. God's people then lead from a Christian leadership perspective in a spirit of discipline and self-denial. Those gifted with leadership abilities are to do it with godly character, all the while looking to mentor and train possible successors.

BE A MOUNTAIN CLIMBER FOR CHRIST

As a Christian, which of Enlow's Seven Mountains will you climb, or encourage others (especially Christian young people) to climb?

- Media Mountain. Media encompasses news outlets, television stations and networks, websites, print media, and radio stations that establish what news is and report it. A key point is media organizations can actually decide what the news is. That is a lot of power. Terror is often carried by these communication organizations. Information is twisted, and bad news fills the airwaves.

- Government Mountain. This mountain, which involves politics, is about administrating civil righteousness and justice. This sector is composed of but not limited to the president, senators, congressman, and other high governmental officials. The corruption must be dealt with and replaced by the influence of God through leaders so His will is accomplished for the nations.

- Education Mountain. This area deals with knowledge or skill obtained by a developmental process. In America, many educational institutions were established and taught from a biblical worldview perspective but not today. Today many universities are filled with liberal minds and information that often replaces God with man. Students are indoctrinated with humanistic views. Enlow believes even Christian universities do not give the proper kingdom perspective to students. This free flow of atheism, liberalism, and rationalism polluting the minds of people needs to stop.

- Economy Mountain. This wealth sector is about the efficient use of resources that includes production, distribution, and consumption. Often there are people in positions of power, who are corrupt, which causes a breakdown in the system.

- Religion Mountain. Religion is about one being in the service and worship of a God or supernatural deity. As Christians, we believe that we serve the one true God that manifests Himself in three ways (Father, Son, and Spirit). The issue of this mountain is to deal with the idolatry (worship of a physical entity as if it were a god; or being excessively attached or devoted to something) of the other major religions of the world, i.e., Islam, Hinduism, and other Chinese faiths (Taoism, Confucianism, and Buddhism). People are stripped of their protection and provision when idolatry reigns in one's life, according to Enlow.

- Celebration Mountain. This sector is comprised of arts, music, sports, fashion, and entertainment. This mountain seems to easily capture and corrupt the hearts and minds of people. Here corruption manifests itself as deception (counterfeiting and perverting what is moral and ethical), and control through things such as lust or sex.

- Family Mountain. The family has been broken down and broken up. The hearts of the fathers are not to their children nor the children to their fathers. Heart revolutions are needed to stop the social injustices. Family mixed with morality is vital for the order of society. When the family is not intact, other issues and injustices can more readily arise.

Leaders are needed on each of these mountains. God's leaders cannot continue to afford to be passive while letting godless, characterless, and demonically inspired men to seize pivotal positions of power.

WHY WE CLIMB MOUNTAINS

George Mallory was a famous English mountaineer who made a failed attempt to summit Mount Everest in 1924. A newspaper reporter asked him why he wanted to climb the treacherous mountain.

"Because it's there," he replied.

Christian leaders have a different motive. We climb and rescue because we have a decree from our Lord to do that. The command to "go and make disciples" rings from the base camp to the mountain peaks.

Servant leaders are not concerned with propagating leaders in their own image. They want to empower leaders in Christ's image. That means helping to empower believers regardless of what mountain God has called them to climb.

What mountains are you climbing today? Who are you teaching to climb with you?

1 2

Who Is Next?

Succession planning and leadership development can be mutually exclusive, but they should not be. This kind of planning and leadership go hand-in-hand.

Perhaps one of the worst examples of succession planning, and one that changed American history in a negative way forever, was when Andrew Johnson succeeded Abraham Lincoln as president after Lincoln's assassination. Lincoln was a Republican who had a plan to restore the Union after the Civil War. Johnson, his vice-president, was a southern Democrat who only wanted to restore the South.

Johnson supported the Union, but it soon became clear that his heart was not in fair-minded reconstruction. Southern legislatures sought to restore their old power structures, and continue to denigrate former slaves. The Republican Congress wanted to invalidate those state elections. Johnson vetoed those bills. He was also against the Fourteenth Amendment to the Constitution, which gave citizenship to freed slaves, and he opposed other civil rights for them.

Abraham Lincoln made a serious error in judgment when he selected a person with a different ideology for his running mate. The United States still suffers from his choice because Johnson denied fair and equitable healing to take place, and the void was filled with racial rancor that is still with us today.

Better succession planning could have changed the destiny of the United States and tens of millions of individuals. But secession was on Lincoln's mind, not succession. Legend has it that he had a dream about his own impending death, but it did not motivate him enough to make sure the right people would take over the reins of power upon his departure.

To ensure the success of an organization for the long term, leadership development should work in tandem with succession planning. When the two are tied together, it enhances the organization's stability because those placed in leadership have been groomed for the task. No leader should be replaced by another who is ill-prepared for the position. Remember, a major function of all leaders is to select and train other leaders.

What is succession planning? It is a strategy for examining current workers. Candidates are carefully selected and intentionally prepared over time to fill leadership positions as they become vacant due to turnover or retirement.

Even when we use contemporary methods to assess qualifications, we keep spiritual principles at the forefront of our thinking. No person is qualified if they fail to meet God's standards as a leader.

William Rothwell, who wrote *Effective Succession Planning*, noted that succession planning is the process that helps stabilize the tenure of personnel and enables the continued effective performance of an organization, division, department, or workgroup by providing for the development, replacement, and strategic use of key people over time. The sad fact is that many churches and ministry organizations do not successfully plan for their future leaders.

Succession programs facilitate the transition of vetted and trained individuals who are already familiar with the mission of the organization to eventually fill positions in leadership. In a process like this, people have the opportunity to validate their skills and giftings over time.

As I have emphasized, the strength of any organization rests on its leaders. Successful succession planning, or the lack thereof, can be the life or death of any ministry or organization. For churches, in particular, every pastor needs to realize that they are an interim pastor. A day will come when every church leader will be replaced.

Due to the lack of succession planning, local churches have suffered. According to Warren Bird, who wrote *Putting 'Success' in Succession*, the now-deceased Pastor Earl Paulk's Chapel Hill Harvester Church is no longer in existence. Pastor Paulk had no successor. Jerry Falwell, founder of Thomas Road Baptist Church, which drew 2000 attendees a week, died of a heart attack in 2007, leaving his son in charge. However, he left no detailed plan of action for the future of the church. The sad fact is the "no plan" plan has been the plan for many an organization. Some pastors ages forty-five to sixty-five may talk about succession, but few actually create a specific plan to accomplish it.

Keep in mind these four common aspects of successful succession planning:

- Focus on the ongoing mission of the organization
- Closely track the development of internal candidates and high potentials
- Consider outside candidates

- Always remember the person needs to "fit" the organization

Every leadership team needs to analyze where the ministry or organization is and where it needs to go. That kind of strategic thinking includes long-range goals, strengths, weaknesses, opportunities, finances, threats, and other organizational dynamics. After internal and external analysis, the leadership should review internal candidates. Their task is to evaluate if any are ready to take on a particular leadership role or be developed to take the helm of preselected positions in the future.

The potential new leaders need to be analyzed for both skill sets, values, and personality to ensure a match for the firm at that designated time. Any basic succession process could take a minimum of two or three years to plan and begin to implement. The time to start actively planning is now. Bringing in a new person is an option in many cases. Hiring replacements from outside the organization can bring a fresh perspective and mind-set but must be done with utmost care.

KEY POSITIONS

For succession planning and execution to be accomplished well, organizational leaders need to identify key positions. A key position influences organizational activities operationally and or strategically. Key positions are primarily recognized for the significance of their role in the organization.

According to Rothwell, key positions can be identified in six ways.

- By the consequences of the position being vacant. If a position is vacant and significant decisions cannot be made, hindering the organization's mission, the result will be holistic negative effects on the organization.

- By creating and defining the organizational chart. When an organizational chart is created, decide which positions significantly contribute to the organization's mission and decide if the specific functions or departments can operate if the leader is gone.

- By questioning. Ask leaders what positions they need filled or else significant problems for the company will be the result.

- By considering historical evidence. Investigate whether the firm would experience significant disruption if there were sudden leadership departures.

- By charting network or decision flow. One should trace the path of communication flow during decisions to decipher who is included, and why some individuals are not included. Identify which individuals are sought after for important decision advice.

- By combining other criteria. Combine two or more of the previous approaches to double-check the validity of the results.

SUCCESSORS

Once key positions are identified, then potential candidates need to be identified and vetted to fill those positions once they are vacated. Consider the significance of selecting a successor from Crystal Cathedral. Alan Hayes, who wrote an article titled "A Transition From Founder to Daughter: The Crystal Cathedral," stated that in June 2009 Senior Pastor Robert H. Schuller announced that his daughter, Sheila Coleman Schuller, would begin directing the church's operations. One problem was Sheila never planned to lead the ministry. One writer said her appointment was the unplanned and undesired conclusion of family disputes.

The family, all still part of Crystal Cathedral Ministries at the time, split with the church in a very public feud with the church's board over theological and financial matters. Eventually, Robert A. Schuller, the son, was made the senior pastor. In 2008, the church's board of directors reduced his authority, making one brother-in-law the chief executive officer and gave another the title of president. These decisions were exacerbated by the pressure of the church's crushing $50 million debt.

According to Hayes, in November of 2008, Robert Schuller was removed from the television broadcast, and then in December 2008, he resigned from the ministry altogether. Later it was revealed that the son wanted to be the weekly preacher, but other family members wanted weekly guest preachers. Robert H. Schuller, the patriarch, later tried to smooth things over by saying there was a lack of shared vision. In 2012, the Crystal Cathedral was sold to the Roman Catholic Diocese of Orange County.

You can see from this how important it is for organizations to select their successors in a clear, methodical process to avoid the faults and failures other organizations have experienced.

CULTURE FIT AND VALUE FIT

To counter Crystal Cathedral-like results, it is better that leadership preselects candidates who would be well-suited to replace outgoing leaders. The team should create a profile and seek a candidate that fits it. Consider using the following information in your evaluation.

CHECK THE HEART

Each organization's leadership needs to use its stated values as a basis for vetting potential people to hire. Rothwell stated that values are beliefs about what is good, bad, or important. Values are filters that shape the way people see the world. They enable what a person takes notice of and how they interpret the data. Those predisposed mind-sets will result in management perceptions, strategic choices, and ultimately personal and organizational performance.

Values are yardsticks for the description, evaluation, and judgment of an individual's thoughts and actions. Leadership is more than just about mental and technical knowledge. It is about character, values, virtues, and standards. Personal values should be the compass that will keep leaders going in the right direction.

Organizations must apply values clarification when it comes to hiring and indoctrinating employees. Values clarification means identifying what values take priority over others. For example, if a family-focused church was looking for another lead pastor, the leadership should not seriously consider hiring a pastor who has had several failed marriages, or is constantly and simultaneously dating others in and out of the church. This pastor obviously would not be a good value or cultural fit. The point is, any group's values should drive strategic and tactical decisions.

WORK EXPERIENCE

Work experience alone is not an indication of leadership ability but does often reveal it. A leader's work experience adds to their leadership credibility or shows a lack of it. The longer a person is in a position, the more one learns about that job. High-potential candidates can illustrate how valuable they are to an organization by noting their relevant job history. These candidates can list a record of promotion and incorporate details, such as teams managed, people led, key projects completed, ministry accomplishments, and more. In today's marketplace, position seekers may have to compete with others who prove their value through measurable metrics-driven achievements.

Leaders can also draw from person-centered psychologist Carl Rogers' childhood experience. He was raised on his family farm, and he witnessed a seed potato develop in the harshest of environments. Those childhood familiarities influenced his view that personal growth is possible even after the darkest of life experiences. No matter what the environment, one can learn and grow. By reviewing a leader's experiences, you can pick up clues if the candidate has had formative situations and circumstances that enlightened, strengthened, and tempered the person through the highs and lows of leadership and life.

POSITION (JOB) DESCRIPTIONS

A job description lists the functions and role responsibilities required for a specific position. All job descriptions should be clear, detailed, accurate, and periodically reviewed in order to remain valid to the person and the role being fulfilled. A typical job description will entail job title, job mission, position within the organization, general context, activities, and expected results.

A position description lays out the essential parts of the job, not a cursory or marginal one. Rothwell noted that position descriptions are advantageous for three reasons.

- Most organizations have them. Many are familiar with job descriptions and understand the need for them.

- Position descriptions can be the basis for making decisions, which include selecting, appraising, and training.

- They provide a foundation of legal evidence of what is necessary to perform the work.

Even faith-based organizations can benefit from these guidelines.

START PLANNING NOW

Statistics reveal that from 40 percent to more than 70 percent of business owners do not have a transition plan. In 2006, a study was conducted and found that out of 2,200 nonprofits, more than 50 percent of them had no succession plan.

This statistic is intensified by demographics. Those born in the post-World War II boom generation, which totaled 78 million, are having problems finding replacements among those in the Generation X group, which totals only an approximate 38 million.

The statistics for churches and organizations is probably far lower. Nevertheless, organizations that suffered a fate similar to the Crystal Cathedral tend to see succession as an event, rather than as a process.

The day a person starts a church or any other entity, he or she should see the inevitable end. This is the essence of succession planning. Once leaders have defined the scope of their duties, they should choose, or at least have a method of choosing, someone who is capable of assuming their role and seamlessly continuing the organization's stated mission.

Information like this should stir leaders to have a succession plan. Has your organization put a succession plan in writing? If not, it should get priority action.

13

Christian Leadership Is Godly Action

Theodore Roosevelt said, "Far better it is to dare mighty things, to win glorious triumphs, even though checkered by failure, than to take rank with those poor spirits who neither enjoy much nor suffer much, because they live in the gray twilight that knows neither victory nor defeat."

Christian leaders understand what Roosevelt was saying. Christian leaders are called to suffering, just as our Lord suffered, yet at the same time we are able to see lives changed and our Lord glorified as a result of our leadership.

Has God been speaking to you about your leadership skills and goals? Depending on where you are in your life and leadership journey, the spiritual principles in this book can be life-changing and organizationally transformational when you apply them. If you have a sense of conviction, longing, aggravation, or frustration in your soul, then God is working in your heart to bring you into alignment with these principles.

You cannot afford to be passive. As a leader or a person who is developing to be a leader, God's plan for your life and faith community is being held up or released, based upon your deliberate action or lack of action. When God is speaking and convicting, it is time for follow-through.

REPRESENT THE KINGDOM

God is calling people to be His image on the earth. He is not only gathering leaders but ones who comprehensively know how to live by God's standards. It is that kind of Christian leadership the Church and the world needs. The Church, the people not the buildings, is God's representative in the earth. God's children are the salt, light, and life of Christ in the earth.

How much more can the church decline and still be effective? That is a shocking question to ask, but an important one to answer. The underlying spiritual problems can only be solved by spiritual men and women using spiritual principles.

In laymen's terms, your lifestyle should be based on beliefs presented in God's Word. The time for you to be a Christian leader is now. Change the way you think, change your perspective, and act like you are the salt God created you to be. Expand God's kingdom by leading as He would.

JUST SERVE PEOPLE

Servant leadership is part of the leadership toolkit a Christian needs to use to help accomplish God's plan on earth. Servant leadership is not the only style or brand of leadership a disciple of Christ embodies, but it is significant since it is one of the main models provided during His earthly ministry.

Christ died for the world and gave the greatest example of servant leadership that can be given. Jesus spent His life serving and guiding others to the place He had called them. God is still calling leaders to serve others as He served them.

No matter if it is preaching, praying, serving food and clothing, providing shelter, directing a team, heading up a business meeting, or any of the numerous duties an executive may have, it is all undergirded by the mind-set to serve the people and look out for their best interests, not the self-interest of the leader. It is about being concerned and preoccupied with the lives of others and building better organizations with them. The goal of the servant leader is to serve others, support others, and deliberately accomplish acts of humility by placing the needs of others before their own. That is the example of Christ that we are charged as Christians to emulate.

DISCIPLINE IS A LIFESTYLE

Don't kid yourself. To be a strong leader, you need to discipline yourself. Paul told Timothy to "train yourself for godliness" (1 Timothy 4:8). That discipline is found in the day-to-day duties, such as accomplishing what you say you would do. Being in charge is not barking out orders to people. It is about mastering yourself and making sure that you're following Christ in word and in deed.

The mark of a mature Christian leader is discipline. Discipline can support and propel your life or be the demise of it. The lack of self-discipline can lead to a lack of follow-through, and that leads to a lack of credibility and trust. God needs His leaders to train themselves with spiritual disciplines by opening their minds and emotions to Him and by having an openness to His directing Spirit.

What is God speaking to you about? What areas need to be reinforced and maintained through godly disciplines, such as prayer, fasting, reading the scriptures, being accountable to godly counsel, and so forth? Stop procrastinating! Put your personal desires aside so you are able to engage fully in enriching your spiritual side.

Allow the Spirit of God to change your leadership profile into the image of Jesus Christ. Leadership development is spiritual formation. Do not run from it. Submit to God's shaping process. God's calling on your life requires discipline if you are to be counted as a "good and faithful servant." To fight discipline is to fight the hand of God.

BE SELF-LED FIRST

Leaders can forget about leading groups of people and having a great influence on others' lives if they are not first exercising self-leadership. Why would anyone follow your word if you do not follow your own words? This means you must command respect and following of yourself in your own heart and mind before you try to command others.

Part of being self-led is to be self-aware. What is God speaking to you about? What are the things that you need to think about in your own heart? Do you know your own proclivities, propensities, tendencies, predispositions, personality bents, and overall strengths and weaknesses?

You have to know yourself first so you can properly lead others. Take the time to rediscover yourself. Take inventory of your own heart. Just because you took a gift and personality inventory ten years ago does not mean you will get the same results now. What parts of the Dark Triad are showing up in your life on a consistent basis? What areas are you proactively going to pray and take decisive action about now? God wants to refine your character to be more like His character.

RESTRICT YOURSELF

Leaders understand the value of self-imposed restrictions. By reflecting on your life, is God speaking to you about any personal, professional, or ministerial boundaries that are being violated? You must guard your heart, but you also need to guard your time, tasks, priorities, relationships, thought life, and organization. Guard against so-called "mission creep" in all areas of your life to maintain your focus and maximize your resources.

For example, it is fine to give to twenty ministries, but would it be better to give to seven while making a more significant contribution and impact on each? Stay focused on the mission God has given you, and do not depart from the course of action God has planned for your life. Stay on course and stay on target.

Sit down with a pad and pencil and list what tasks, objectives, and distractions you need to give up to get back to the God-ordained direction for your life and organization. Always strive to keep in mind the "Whys" of what you are doing.

LEADERS DEVELOP LEADERS

Biblically speaking, a part of the call to lead is also the call to develop others. You may not be in a direct training role, but it is innately part of what you are equipped by God to do in the earth. Godly leaders need to train up other godly leaders. When you enter a vocation, you need to look for a replacement so you can move on when the time arrives. That is the leadership principle of 2 Timothy 2:2. Paul explained to Timothy that he needed to entrust spiritual principles to reliable people, and that included behavioral as well as doctrinal matters. We teach with our actions as well as our words.

What are you going to start doing now to prepare the baton to be passed to the next leader? Look for protégés, apprentices, understudies, or whatever name you chose to label them. The strength of the Body of Christ rests on its leaders. Stop thinking you have time. Tomorrow is not promised to any man. Today is the day and now is the time to train others how to be fathers, mothers, executives, leaders, and great representatives for Christ.

LEADERSHIP TO CHANGE THE WORLD

God calls those gifted with leadership to be environmentalists. Not an environmentalist in the traditional sense, but one that sets the culture, environment, and atmosphere in a particular setting. The impact of a person representing God, coupled with being in a prominent role, should have a domino effect. That includes the culture of one's organizations. The environment should tell people that once they are under the tutelage of godly leadership, they will be charged to learn and mature in their duties and life. What environment are you creating or supporting? God expects change, and so should those He has called to be leaders. God has an eternal perspective on things, but too many leaders suffer from tunnel vision.

Christians should be involved in every major sector of society to learn, live, and lead for the purposes of Christ. As we know, God's children are salt and light, and if leaders do not develop others to take influential and prominent places in society, the enemy will fill that gap. We see this on a routine basis with the persecution of the church, the moral decay across the nations, and all the incivility and injustice.

Is there hope for the future? Yes. But it requires that God-inspired leaders look into their own souls and question their own motives. None can be guilty of self-aggrandizement. If we are kings as Christian leaders, it is only so we can throw our crowns at the feet of Jesus (Revelation 4:10).

We must confess the sin that Christian leadership is restricted to the church. Our insular approach has failed God. Christian leadership is a spiritual dynamic that has no walls. Christian leaders must use their gifts in all sectors of society, including business, education, the military, and government.

The key to this concept of servant leadership is that we are charged to teach others to be spiritual leaders. There are two terms that go hand-in-hand, and they are *discipline* and *disciple*. We not only discipline ourselves as leaders, as I have described, but we must simultaneously disciple others with the biblical concept of servant leadership. That leadership principle is what Jesus Christ used to change the world, and it is our solemn obligation to honor His motives and methods in our leadership today.

"GO YE"

Christian leadership is light in the darkness. Jesus was clear about our stewardship of that light. He said, "You are the light of the world. A city set on a hill cannot be hidden. Nor do people light a lamp and put it under a basket, but on a stand, and it gives light to all in the house. In the same way, let your light shine before others, so that they may see your good works and give glory to your Father who is in heaven." (Matthew 5:14–16).

All Christians are to be light in this dark world, but Christian leaders have a responsibility to illuminate the way for other believers. That means Christian leaders cannot ruminate for long about the meaning of leadership. They must take action and lead.

Thus, it is not surprising to us that the culminating activity for all of the teaching and preaching that Jesus did was the sending of spiritually disciplined people into spiritual battle.

Just before His ascension, Jesus looked at His personally trained leaders and told them, "All authority in heaven and on earth has been given to me. Go therefore and make disciples of all nations, baptizing them in the name of the Father and of the Son and of the Holy Spirit, teaching them to observe all that I have commanded you. And behold, I am with you always, to the end of the age" (Matthew 28:18–20).

Jesus is speaking to you. He has chosen you as a leader and He wants you to put your leadership gifts and skills into action now. Start by exercising self-leadership and use it to help bring change to others. Use Christian leadership to change the world.

Bibliography

Andersen, Roger. *The Executive Calling*. Creation House, Lake Mary, FL, 2008.

Bird, Warren. "Putting 'Success' in Succession: Prominent Pastors Go Public with How to Wisely Pass the Leadership Baton." *Christianity Today*, vol. 58, no. 9, Nov. 2014, pp. 50–53. EBSCOhost.

Calhoun, Adele A. *Spiritual Disciplines Handbook: Practices that Transform Us*. InterVarsity Press, Westmont, 2015.

Castelli, Patricia A. "Reflective Leadership Review: A Framework for Improving Organisational Performance." *Journal of Management Development*, vol. 35, no. 2, 2016, pp. 217–236.

Clinton, Robert. *The Making of a Leader: Recognizing the Lessons and Stages of Leadership Development*. Tyndale House Publishers, Inc., 2018.

Cloud, Henry. *Boundaries for Leaders: Results, Relationships, and being Ridiculously in Charge*. HarperBusiness, New York, NY, 2013.

Cloud, Henry, and John S. Townsend. *Boundaries: When to Say Yes, when to Say No to Take Control of Your Life*. Zondervan Pub. House, Grand Rapids, MI, 2004.

Enlow, Johnny. *The Seven Mountain Prophecy: Unveiling the Coming Elijah Revolution*. Charisma Media, 2008.

Eric Rust. "Self Leadership: Leading From the Inside Out."

Furtner, Marco R., John F. Rauthmann, and Pierre Sachse. "Unique Self-Leadership: A Bifactor Model Approach." Leadership 11, no. 1 (2015): 105–125.

Geiger, Eric, and Kevin Peck. *Designed to Lead: The Church and Leadership Development.* B&H Publishing Group, 2016.

Goleman, Daniel. "The Focused Leader." Harvard Business Review 91.12 (2013): 50–60.

Jakobwitz, Sharon, and Vincent Egan. "The Dark Triad and Normal Personality Traits." Personality and Individual Differences, vol. 40, no. 2, 2006, pp. 331–339.

Kouzes, James M., and Barry Z. Posner. *The Leadership Challenge.* Jossey-Bass, San Francisco, CA, 2012.

Lichtenstein, Scott. "The Role of Values in Leadership: How Leaders' Values Shape Value Creation." *Integral Leadership Review* 12.3 (2012).

Manning, J. *The Disciplines Leader: Keeping the Focus on what Really Matters*, Berrett-Koehler Publishers Inc. Oakland, CA, 2015.

Matsuo, Makoto. "Reflective Leadership and Team Learning: An Exploratory Study." *Journal of Workplace Learning*, vol. 28, no. 5, 2016, pp. 307–321.

McIntosh, Gary, L., Rima, Samuel, D. *Overcoming the Dark Side of Leadership.* Baker Books, Grand Rapids, MI, 2008.

Patterson, Kathleen A. *Servant Leadership: A Theoretical Model.* Dissertation, Regent University, 2003.

Popov, Stanislava, Miklos Biro, and Jelena Radanovic. "Self-Evaluation and Mental Health: An Experimental Assessment." *Journal of Evidence-Based Psychotherapies,* vol. 15, no. 2, 2015, p. 219.

Rodriguez, Samuel. *Be Light: Shining God's Beauty, Truth, and Hope in a Darkened World.* WaterBrook Press. Colorado Springs, Colorado. 2016.

Rothwell, William. *Effective Succession Planning: Ensuring Leadership Continuity and Building Talent from Within.* Amacom, New York, NY. 2010.

Schein, Edgar H. *Organizational Culture and Leadership.* Vol. 2. John Wiley & Sons, 2010.

Stringer, Doug. *Leadership Awakening: Fundamental Principles for Lasting Success.* Whitaker House. New Kensington, PA. 2016.

Taylor, Richard S. *The Disciplined Life: The Mark of Christian Maturity.* Bethany House Publishers, Bloomington, Minnesota, 1962.

Velsor, Ellen V., Cynthia D. McCauley, and Marian N. Ruderman. *The Center for Creative Leadership Handbook of Leadership Development.* Jossey-Bass, Hoboken, NJ, 2010.

OTHER SOURCES

Christian Character Score

DellaVecchio Motivational Gifts Survey

Neris Analytics Personality Inventory

American Addiction Centers. https://americanaddictioncenters.org/

Robert Greenleaf. https://www.greenleaf.org/

The Barna Group. https://www.barna.com/

The Pew Research Center. https://www.pewresearch.org/

About the Author

Dr. Rickardo Bodden serves as the chief operating officer and an associate pastor of a leading ministry in the Washington, DC Metropolitan Area. He has an earned doctorate in strategic leadership from Regent University, a master of arts degree in psychology of leadership from Bellevue University, and a bachelor of science degree in mass communication from Florida International University.

Prior to his current positions, Dr. Bodden served in the United States Air Force in several public relations and communication leadership positions at stateside and overseas locations. As a corporate communication professional, he led teams in accomplishing organizational goals through employee communication, reputation management, crisis response communication, issues management, and media and community engagement.

All of his personal and professional experiences have helped create the bedrock of his personal philosophy: self-leadership is the basis for all leadership. Dr. Bodden continues to mentor, coach, and develop the people around him. His passion is to see leaders grow beyond personal limitations to be the leader God has ordained.